happiness
works

jessica weiss

happiness works

the science of

**thriving
at
work**

WILEY

Published by John Wiley & Sons, Inc., Hoboken, New Jersey.
Published simultaneously in Canada.

For general information on our other products and services or for technical support, please contact our Customer Care Department within the United States at (800) 762-2974, outside the United States at (317) 572-3993 or fax (317) 572-4002.

Wiley also publishes its books in a variety of electronic formats. Some content that appears in print may not be available in electronic formats. For more information about Wiley products, visit our web site at www.wiley.com.

Library of Congress Cataloging-in-Publication Data is Available:

ISBN 9781394329182 (Cloth)
ISBN 9781394329205 (ePub)
ISBN 9781394329212 (ePDF)

COVER ART & DESIGN: PAUL MCCARTHY
Printed and bound by CPI Group (UK) Ltd, Croydon, CR0 4YY

C9781394329182_120925

For My Grandparents:

To Grandma Esther, whose laughter I can still hear every day

To Grandpa Aron, whose kindness taught me how a gentle heart can transform the world around it

To Grandma Hana, whose unconditional love never wavered

And to Grandpa Marcus, whose stories planted the seeds of this very book

Though you are no longer here to hold these pages in your hands, I feel your pride radiating through time. This book exists because you existed, because you believed in dreams and in me. I write these words wrapped in the warmth of your memory, knowing somewhere, Grandma is laughing in delight at what her grandchild has accomplished.

Your legacy lives on in these pages.

With eternal gratitude and love,

Jessi

Contents

Introduction
Work That Works

Imagine that you are 24 minutes into a mind-numbing conference call when you see this Post-it Note on your colleague's cubicle wall: "Do what you love and you'll never work a day in your life!"

Did you nearly choke on your coffee?

We've all been there, watching the minutes of our life tick away while Bob from accounting drones on about quarterly projections, and this cheerful yellow square is mocking us with its empty promises. If that Post-it Note wisdom were true, why are 67 percent of Americans actively disengaged at work? Why are millions of us living for the weekend and drowning in "Sunday Scaries"?

"Follow your passion and the money will follow" belongs in the same fantasy land. Look, I've interviewed thousands of workers, and I can tell you with absolute certainty: These mantras aren't just misleading; they're downright harmful. They've created a generation of professionals who believe happiness at work is something you stumble into rather than something you build.

The Myth of the Dream Job

Let me tell you about David, a software engineer who spent seven years job-hopping through four different tech companies. Each time, the pattern was identical: initial excitement about new challenges, followed by a honeymoon period of about six months, then the slow creep of familiar dissatisfaction.

"I kept thinking the next company would be different," David told me during our interview. "Better culture, more inspiring mission, cooler perks. But after the fourth job change, I realized that I was bringing the same mindset, the same habits, and the same expectations to each new environment."

David isn't alone. The "dream job fallacy" affects millions of professionals who believe their unhappiness stems from being in the wrong job rather than from how they approach their work. The problem with this is that it places the responsibility for your happiness entirely outside your control—in the hands of employers, managers, and arbitrary circumstances.

The data tells a different story. In my research spanning industries from healthcare to manufacturing to technology, I found something surprising: People with nearly identical job descriptions, working for the same companies, often reported wildly different levels of satisfaction. Some thrived while others languished, despite facing the same external conditions.

So what separated the flourishers from the flounderers? It wasn't salary, title, or even the specifics of their day-to-day tasks. It was their approach.

We live in a culture that's obsessed with defining people by their jobs. Think about it—what's the first question you hear at a party? "So . . . what do you do for a living?" As if that single answer will tell you everything worth knowing about a person. This isn't just smalltalk; it reflects American society's deep-rooted belief that our work should be our identity, our purpose, and our passion all rolled into one.

But here's the truth I've discovered after 15 years of research: Being happy at work has surprisingly little to do with "following your passion." It's much more nuanced than that—and thankfully much more within your control than you might think. The path to workplace happiness isn't about finding the perfect job; it's about developing the right skills to thrive in the job you have.

The Cost of Workplace Unhappiness

Before we dive into solutions, let's acknowledge what's at stake. Workplace unhappiness isn't just a minor inconvenience—it exacts a tremendous toll on our lives.

The average American spends roughly 90,000 hours at work over their lifetime. That's about a third of your waking existence. When you're unhappy at work, that unhappiness doesn't stay neatly contained within office hours. It seeps into your relationships, your health, and your overall sense of well-being.

Studies have linked workplace dissatisfaction to everything from increased risk of heart disease and depression to shortened lifespan. The stress hormones released during a miserable Monday don't magically disappear when you clock out. They continue circulating, affecting your sleep, your immune system, and even your cognitive function.

Then there's the opportunity cost—all the moments of potential joy, creativity, and fulfillment that never materialize because you're just trying to survive until Friday. The family dinners where you're physically present but mentally still replaying that contentious meeting. The hobbies you abandon because you're too emotionally drained to engage with them.

This isn't just philosophical—it's practical. When we resign ourselves to workplace unhappiness, we're making a devastating trade: sacrificing our present well-being for a future that may never arrive in the form we imagine.

The Happiness Framework: Building from the Ground Up

This book isn't about magic formulas or quick fixes. What I offer instead is something more valuable: a proven framework that builds the foundations of genuine workplace satisfaction from the ground up.

The secret I've discovered after years of research is that happiness isn't a threshold that you cross where everything changes. It emerges naturally when you develop traits like efficacy, resilience, optimism, and empathy. These qualities don't just make work bearable—they make it meaningful and fulfilling.

When you cultivate these habits, you start recognizing happiness when it appears in your day. You stop missing those moments of joy that once passed you by unnoticed. The goal isn't constant contentment—that's not realistic or desirable.

With the right perspective, even a routine meeting can become an opportunity for connection. A challenging project transforms into a chance for growth. A setback becomes a valuable lesson that propels you forward. These are fundamental shifts in how you experience your work life.

Beyond Self-Help Clichés: Real Solutions for Real People

This framework isn't about morning meditation routines or keeping a gratitude journal at your desk (though if those work for you, fantastic). I won't suggest that scented candles or desktop plants will solve structural problems in your workplace. What I offer instead are evidence-based strategies that address the root causes of workplace unhappiness.

My framework focuses on five core areas that research consistently shows are essential to workplace satisfaction. For each area, I'll offer many practical approaches so you can choose what works best for your unique situation. Some will be small adjustments you can implement immediately; others will be more substantial changes that require time and practice. All of them have been proven effective across industries, roles, and personality types.

Throughout the book, you'll meet people from all walks of life who have transformed their experience at work, without changing jobs—people like Maria, a senior policy analyst at a large insurance company.

When I met her, Maria told me she used to really enjoy her job, but she hadn't felt that way in a while. A number of things had changed.

Her best friend at work left for another job—leaving a void in Maria's days that she hadn't been able to fill. Her last two big projects had fizzled, making her start to doubt her own abilities. A new management team had told her to "go back to the drawing board" and she wasn't sure what was expected of her anymore. People on her team were becoming defensive and starting to play the "blame game" with each other.

She was feeling anxious and trapped. She had lost all of her happiness at work. She no longer felt that satisfaction or contentment. She didn't know how to get her happiness back. But she ultimately did.

Stories like these will show you that happiness at work isn't reserved for the lucky few who stumble into dream careers. It's available to anyone willing to approach their work with intention and purpose.

If you've ever felt that creeping dread on Sunday evenings or wondered if there's more to work than just surviving until retirement, this book is for you. Consider it the conversation I wish someone had started with me years ago—an invitation to think differently about happiness at work.

Not as an unattainable ideal reserved for a select few, but as a practical, achievable reality that we can create together, one day at a time.

Are you ready to take control of your happiness at work? Let's begin.

Introduction

Chapter 1

Why Aren't You Happy at Work?

A re *you* happy at work?

Imagine this. You are sitting in a room full of people, all neatly dressed and looking successful, coffee cups in hand. I stand before them and ask one simple question: "Are you happy at work?"

The silence is deafening. Awkward glances bounce around the room. A few nervous laughs break the tension.

I've posed this question to thousands of people across industries, job titles, and salaries. The result? A sea of hesitation, with only rare islands of genuine enthusiasm.

Why?

What invisible force has turned our workplaces—where we spend a third of our adult lives—into zones of quiet desperation? Why do Monday mornings trigger dread rather than excitement? Why do so many of us count down to Friday while wishing away precious hours of our finite existence?

This isn't just about job satisfaction. It's about a profound disconnect between what work could be and what it has become.

What's interesting is that this is not a new problem: People have been complaining about their jobs for as long as people have had jobs to go to (Aristotle was asking what it was all for more than two thousand years ago). In 1962, researchers conducted a survey that asked Americans: "What is the formula for success?" Six percent of people cited meaningful work as being part of the formula.[1]

They conducted the exact same survey 20 years later and they found that 49 percent of people believed that meaningful work was part of success. Today 90 percent of Americans would take a pay cut just to find a bit more happiness at work.[2]

Sure, the COVID pandemic is part of that story, but the data shows that reasons for unhappiness run much deeper. In 2021, 47 million Americans quit their job.[3] Years later, while quit rates have begun to normalize (although still historically high), 46 percent of people are thinking about quitting their jobs. That's *more* people than the 40 percent who said this in 2021.[4]

And then there's "quiet quitting" or "career cushioning" (that's preparing for a job change while you're still employed), when the "Great Resignation" transitioned into the "Great Renegotiation." (Memo to the media: Is any of this really "great"?) While the data is harder to come by on this trend, it's clear that many people are focusing on the *quality* of their jobs.

The reality of the pandemic is that it gave us time to pause and reflect, often for the first time in a long time. People are thinking more about what they want from work. It was a moment of reckoning, and suddenly, having a fancy job title doesn't seem all that important to many of us.

What people want instead is satisfaction and contentment from their work.

In some ways, it's a simple story: Forced to face our mortality, many of us decided to no longer accept the status quo. While people used to think of being unhappy at work as "normal," a lot of us now believe that we deserve better. That we deserve to be happy at work.

This is a moment for every organization to listen, to adapt, to change, and to improve. Companies must take the time to understand why employees are leaving. The pandemic showed us that we all want a more human place to work. We want our employers to take into account our mental health, our physical health, and our overall well-being. Organizations that do this well—and act thoughtfully—will have an edge in attracting and retaining talent.

Here's the good news: It's more possible than you think. For many decades now, people have been studying how to make work more satisfying and we have real science-backed insights and tools that are *proven* to work. Yes, proven to work.

By building up specific habits, tools, and strategies, I will show you how we can get better at being happy at work. And guess what? It's not that complicated and it's not that hard. We'll be spending most of the book diving into these insights, learning the tactical things that have been scientifically shown to make a real difference.

The Secret Ingredient for Success

Curious about something even more encouraging? Many still view happiness as a luxury rather than a necessity, prioritizing salary over satisfaction. What they don't recognize is that workplace happiness is precisely what leads to greater financial rewards. In fact, happiness isn't just beneficial—it's the fundamental element that determines your success.

In fact, happiness is the secret ingredient for success. I believe that when people are happy at work, they will go on to achieve extraordinary things for the companies that they work for. I believe business has the capacity to create a more equitable and happier world.

Happiness is a serious tool for business. The happier your employees, the happier your customers, the more successful your business will be. And the truth is that there is a lot of evidence now that says the most successful organizations, the ones with a happy and engaged work force, are more profitable and more productive, with fewer sick days and lower turnover. If you care about your people and what makes them happy at work, your customers and clients will get better service and you will have a more successful business.

It's true. Study after study has shown this.

A Gallup meta-analysis of 3.3 million employees in 112 countries found that happy teams were 18 percent more productive and had 81 percent less absenteeism.[5] A Harvard study showed that happy employees produced 37 percent higher sales and were three times more creative.[6] A study of 25 years of stock market data showed that companies with high employee satisfaction outperformed their peers by 3.7 percent annually—in other words, those companies that valued satisfaction and happiness at work produced double the value of the unhappy ones over that time period.[7]

These studies are all showing the same thing: It's not that success makes people happy, but that happiness makes them successful. Their happiness creates the conditions for achievement, advancement, and fulfillment.

How do we know this? To start, we can look at the characteristics of those people who love their work and see how those characteristics make them successful. Take just a few examples:

- **Better cognitive performance:** Having a positive mindset makes it easier for us to think and focus. Happy people show improved memory and decision-making, which leads to better problem-solving abilities.

- **Increased resilience:** Happy employees are more likely to persist when facing a challenge, which means that they bounce back from setbacks faster than other people. This makes them better able to withstand tough situations.

- **Stronger relationships:** Happy people are well-liked by their peers. This makes them better at building and maintaining professional networks, and more likely to receive mentorship and support.

- **More ambition:** Happy people tend to be more motivated and set higher goals for themselves. This often leads to more positive evaluations, more frequent promotions, and a higher chance of being picked for leadership roles.

I'm sure we'd all like to experience these benefits, whether they make us happier or not. (Fortunately, they do.) The important message is that happiness is not a fluke. It is within your control. The goal of this book is to give you, and your team, the tools to take control of your own happiness and become more successful in your career.

Four Reasons You're Not Happy at Work

You're probably asking yourself: If we know that being happy will make us more successful, why aren't more of us doing it? Why does it feel so difficult? What's the problem here?

I've spent the last 15 years listening to people tell me why they are unhappy in their jobs and studying the people who *are* happy and successful. At first, I was part of a large management consulting firm that would go into major corporations and work with teams to remove barriers to their success. Before long, fascinated by what I was hearing, I launched my own consultancy focused specifically on employee and team happiness. I did extensive interviews and sent out detailed surveys to dig into what triggered and prevented people from being happy at work. At the same time, I was coaching individuals on how to be happier in their careers, listening to their complaints and building concrete action plans that saw them become both happier and more successful over time.

I'll share some of these stories throughout the book. But what I saw over and over again is that **people are doing the wrong things to be happy**.

There's a lot of conventional wisdom around career success and happiness that is just plain wrong. This often leads people to pursue

5

things that do not improve their happiness, or have even been proven to *negatively* affect it. Other times, people decide that happiness is not in their control and they resign themselves to suffering without even trying to change.

That's why, before we get into the concrete steps you can take to make you and your teams happier at work, I want to debunk some of the common myths that people pursue. By showing why these strategies do not lead to happiness, I want you to remove some of the common obstacles that can get in your way and eliminate the behaviors that are making you less happy.

Myth 1: More Money Will Make You Happier

We've all been told some version of this from a very young age:

> *Go to school. Study hard. Get a good job. Climb the ladder. Make a bunch of money. And THEN you will be happy.*

And hey, there's some truth to it. You do need to make a certain amount of money to feel safe and secure. It's hard to be happy if you can't pay your bills. But the amount of money you need is probably less than you think.

The problem with tying your happiness to the size of your paycheck is that you're relying on an external source of motivation. And external things are not in our control.

So what should you pursue instead of money? The short answer is that you need to look for things that bring you lasting happiness. You need to be paying attention to internal motivations.

What the Research Says

When you get a raise or promotion at work, you do get happier—for a little while. Research shows that you get a happiness "bump" that will last for . . . maybe six months (if you're lucky). When the anticipated event does happen, you get a little boost of dopamine and serotonin.[8]

Then you pretty quickly go back to your baseline, and start looking for something to bring the happiness back. The goal posts move and you decide that something else (a bigger raise or spending that new money) is needed to feel happy. This is why a lot of people fall into the trap of climbing the corporate ladder, thinking that higher rungs will unlock a new level of happiness. As you get higher up, these dopamine bumps become further and further apart and eventually you run into a ceiling. There's nothing wrong with going after a promotion, but it's not the only key to happiness.

Even worse, the act of seeking an external reward will make you less happy. A fascinating study of a kindergarten class shows why.

Researchers recruited kids who already loved to draw and divided them into three groups:

- Group 1 was promised a "good player award" for drawing.
- Group 2 was given a surprise award after drawing.
- In group 3, no award was mentioned or given.

Two weeks later, the results were revealing. While groups 2 and 3 continued drawing at their usual rate, the first group (those promised rewards) showed significantly less interest in drawing. The external reward had actually diminished their natural love for drawing.[9]

Why am I telling you about children? Children are completely untainted. They haven't been influenced by all the "shoulds" and rules. They are pure little humans who can tell us so much about ourselves.

Similar studies with adults consistently show that when we rely solely on external motivators (raises, promotions, recognition), we risk depleting our internal drive—our sustainable source of motivation.

The irony is that the short-term happiness bump we get after a raise has little to do with the money itself. When you're starting out, the money is making you *less unhappy* by doing away with problems. Then, as you reach a "fair" salary, it's actually the recognition that affects happiness more than pay.[10]

What You Can Do

Despite the mountain of evidence that external validation doesn't work, it's hard to go against a story we've been told since childhood. If you live in the United States, you know that "What do you do?" is often the first question people ask each other when they meet. We're conditioned to believe that a good job leads to happiness. That's why I've had countless conversations with people who've worked hard for years to accomplish a goal, like a new job with a bigger paycheck—and a month later they're telling me, "Jessica, I hate this job. I want to quit. I need a new job."

It's not that making more money is a bad thing. It's just the wrong goal. By focusing on one thing (money) that you have limited control over, you're ignoring all the other proven things you could be doing to make yourself happier.

Instead, focus on internal motivators as a more dependable source of happiness. Intrinsic motivators don't just make people perform better; they also make work more fulfilling. Think about *wanting* to read a book and *having* to read a book—one of those is a lot easier. (And more fun, right?)

We need to look for opportunities to bring intrinsic motivation into our jobs. This means reflecting on what motivates you and asking your teammates what motivates them. It means connecting with your "why"—why, beyond the money, have you chosen to do the work that you do? (We'll talk more about this in Chapter 6.)

If you're a leader, it means creating an environment where intrinsic motivation can flourish. We'll talk more about how to do this in Chapter 9.

Myth 2: Happiness Is a Choice

One of the things that drives me crazy is when people say that they'll just "choose to be happy."

Sorry, but it doesn't work that way. Happiness is not a light switch.

If you think about it for a minute, happiness *can't* be as easy as "deciding" it will happen. If that were true, why wouldn't we all just choose to be happy all the time? You can trick yourself into putting on a happy face for a short time, but it's not a recipe for lasting happiness.

Still, it's not hard to see why people like this idea. It's easy. It gives you the illusion of control. It doesn't take any work. Of course, that's exactly why it's wrong.

The feeling you get from "deciding to be happy" is ephemeral. It doesn't last because it's not built on a solid foundation. It tends to disappear at the first sign of trouble, because it doesn't have the strength to withstand ill winds.

So why do people say this? The problem comes from not understanding what happiness really means. It's not a fleeting feeling that comes and goes; it's something deeper. It's something you build up over time, by practicing the right habits, so that your happiness becomes sustainable, long-lasting, and hard to blow away.

What the Research Says

Decades worth of research shows, over and over, that you cannot simply will yourself to happiness. It can even tell us why.

You may have heard of a "negativity bias." This is the tendency, of the vast majority of people, to respond more to negative things than to positive. It's the reason you remember insults more than compliments, are more hurt by traumas than helped by triumphs, and are more motivated by avoiding pain than seeking gain.

This bias serves an important purpose. Thousands of years ago, noticing bad things quickly was an important survival mechanism. When one wrong move means that you could end up as some animal's dinner, you want to detect danger as soon as possible. This instinct protects you. The people who had this instinct survived more often than those who didn't. Fast forward a few thousand years and evolution has given us a finely tuned radar for paying attention to things that may go wrong.

Unfortunately, this works against us today. The genes of all those hawk-eyed survivors passed down a sensitivity to negativity that's no longer so helpful in the modern world.

The implications of this can be a little hard to swallow. It means that we are not wired for happiness. In some ways, we're wired for the opposite.

What You Can Do

Fortunately, another characteristic of our brains can come to the rescue here: neuroplasticity.

Neuroplasticity is the ability of our brains to change over time. Literally, they can be rewired to learn new behaviors. This means that you can do concrete things to overcome that negativity bias and start to rewire your brain for happiness.

While you can't simply will yourself to long-lasting happiness, you can learn how to cultivate positive emotions.

In 2004, the psychologist Barbara Fredrickson published what became known as the "broaden and build" theory of happiness.

In a nutshell, it states that creating positive emotions can broaden how we respond to events (for example, stop us from jumping to a negative conclusion), which helps us build resilience and cope with negative emotions. By making it easier to call up positive emotions, it makes those feelings more available alongside the negative feelings we experience when faced with a difficult situation.[11]

Essentially, Fredrickson is suggesting that we add small doses of positive energy throughout our day. I call this practical optimism. The purpose is to develop a positive mindset that can withstand the negative emotions that we inevitably experience. It's giving our brain a few well-worn positive circuits that can fire as easily as the negative ones we're wired for.

Here's a few examples of what I mean by positive emotions you can cultivate:

- **Interest:** Develop a sense of curiosity about other people's work. This can help you learn new things and help others by offering them feedback.

- **Inspiration:** Inspiration is the highway to innovation. By putting in the effort to seek out inspiration, you'll find new solutions to problems.

- **Gratitude:** Celebrate your wins and don't take the help of others for granted.

- **Pride:** Give yourself credit for work well done.

Giving yourself permission to feel these emotions, and even seeking them out, is a choice you can make that will lead you to sustainable happiness. (We'll spend Chapter 7 looking at ways to boost your practical optimism.)

Myth 3: Working Less Will Make You Happier

"I would be happier if I could just work less."

You know the fantasy: A pile of money lands in your lap, you move to a tropical island, and life is bliss. No one expects to achieve this dream, but it speaks to a belief that more leisure (a lot more) equals more happiness.

It's true that in the United States we work more hours than people do in many other rich countries. And as we'll see, some of those places where they work a few hours a week less than Americans do rank higher for happiness. But that's just part of the story.

It's what you do with that extra time that matters. So pursuing more time off or a sabbatical (or even a four-day work week) may make you happier—if you use that time doing the things that are proven to help you build happiness.

Also, surprisingly, there is such a thing as *too much* time off. There's a sweet spot for the ideal amount of free time, and the data shows that too much time off can be just as bad for your happiness as not enough. So hold off buying property on that tropical island.

What the Research Says

Cassie Holmes is a professor at UCLA's Anderson School of Management and the author of the book *Happier Hour*. What her research found is that there's a Goldilocks zone for how much free time helps you to be happier. If you have this amount of free time on a daily basis, you have achieved what she calls "time affluence."

What is this perfect amount of time richness? Two to five hours a day.

I know even two hours a day of free time sounds like a lot. If you don't have it, you will probably feel stressed. So if you have a challenging job and a busy home life, finding more time in the day will help you. It's good to keep in mind, however, that this doesn't need to be two continuous hours—if you can find half an hour in the morning, another half hour in the afternoon, and an hour in the evening, that works.

Interestingly, too much free time was just as bad as too little. If you don't have much to show for how you spent your day, you'll lack a sense of purpose and feel dissatisfied. We are meant to be productive.

What You Can Do

Rather than dreaming of a tropical paradise, take control of your day. Use time as a way to build happiness:

- Protect your time for those things that feel worthwhile to you.
- Really enjoy, savor, and make the most of the activities that you love.
- Make time for the work that matters and find time to do that every day.

What you do in those two to five hours matters. Instead of focusing on the time you don't have, aim to spend the time you do have more strategically.

This means organizing your days to include less of what hampers your happiness, more of what matters, and just enough time to do nothing at all. In other words, with a few schedule adjustments, you might be able to find your downtime sweet spot.

One way to build time affluence is to take a task that usually feels like drudgery and turn it into something new. Learning and novelty are powerful tools for increasing happiness. When you're doing something new, your interest spikes and your senses sharpen. You quickly become engaged in what you're doing.

On the other hand, if you're doing the same task over and over, it's easy to feel like you're caught in a Groundhog Day loop and time is passing you by. But if you take that same task and learn a new (maybe even better) way to do it, time feels like it's expanding and is better spent.

Another strategy, which we'll spend much of Chapter 3 diving into, is connecting with another human being. As you look at your to-do list, you might think, "I don't have 15 minutes to meet that new coworker for coffee." But research shows that taking that time to engage with someone, and maybe even help them so that you feel like you've made an impact on their life, will increase your happiness. It will also make you feel like you have more time, because you've accomplished something meaningful.

One of my favorite studies on this topic shows that if a doctor (as time-starved a person as you'll ever find) takes an extra 60 seconds to connect with a patient—ask about their life and show some interest in them as a person—it benefits the patient *and* the doctor. The patient feels like "That doctor has time for me" and the doctor feels like "Oh, I've connected with this person in a meaningful way." That *one minute* makes a huge difference.[12]

If you look for them, you'll find that there are many of these "micro-opportunities" throughout your day. There's even a fantastic term for them: time confetti.

The idea, first expressed by Brigid Schulte in her book *Overwhelmed*, is that we have many of these 5- or 10-minute windows sprinkled throughout the day. If we spend that time mindlessly scrolling our email or social media, that time is wasted and doesn't feel good. But if you use that time to focus on activities that bring us happiness, it feels like recovering lost time.

Myth 4: Happiness Is Genetic and There's Nothing You Can Do About It

When I start working with a team, inevitably someone will pipe up and say, "I'm just not a happy person. I was born that way and there isn't much I can do about it."

I have heard this time and time again.

My answer is always the same: "You're wrong."

There is a problem with how we think about happiness.

Take a study conducted by social scientists at the University of Minnesota. The study looked at 81 pairs of identical twins (and 56 pairs of fraternal twins) who were born between the mid-1930s and the 1950s, separated at birth, and adopted by separate families. People love to ask me, "Jessica, why were they separated at birth?" I have no idea, and it seems odd to me as well, but for the purposes of this story let's just leave that to the side for a minute.

But here's the good news: At the age of 40, these twins were reunited and given personality tests. Now, let's take a step back for a moment. What we have here is a researcher's goldmine. We have twins—two people with identical genetic material—but with completely different upbringings. We can really see what is nature and what is nurture.

What these researchers found is great news for all of us: It turns out that only half of our happiness comes from genetics. But the other half of our happiness is entirely up to us; it's entirely within our control.[13]

The half of our happiness that is determined by our genetics is sometimes referred to as our happiness set point. This means that, without those intentional activities, our level of happiness will generally drift back to the level of happiness that we were born with. This is why, when you get that raise, your happiness only increases for a fairly short period of time.

15

Why Aren't You Happy at Work?

What the Research Says

One of the most famous studies in social science is the Harvard Study of Adult Development. The study has been running for more than 85 years (since 1938), when scientists began tracking the health of 268 second-year students (all men, since Harvard didn't accept female students back then). Those students included future President John F. Kennedy and the legendary editor of *The Washington Post*, Ben Bradlee. As the original cohort passed away, researchers began to include the men's offspring, bringing the total number of subjects to more than 1,300.

Knowing that this was not a typical group of research subjects, in the 1970s the scientists added members of the "Glueck study," made up of 456 inner-city Boston young men who came from what they considered to be disadvantaged or troubled families, as a control group. (Researchers eventually added the spouses of both groups to the project.) The researchers checked in with both groups every two years, asking them questions about their lives and their mental and emotional wellness. They continuously compared the health and happiness of the two groups so they could isolate the impact of socioeconomics.

What they found was that it wasn't money, IQ, or even genetics that led to the best outcomes for people. The single biggest factor impacting happiness *for both groups* was having healthy relationships.

One of the study's startling conclusions was that the quality of subjects' relationships at age 50 was a better predictor of health outcomes than anything else. "The people who were the most satisfied in their relationships at age 50 were the healthiest at age 80."[14]

What You Can Do

The Harvard Study of Adult Development shows that a significant part of our happiness is within our control and cultivating healthy relationships is a great place to start. We'll do a deep dive on how to strengthen your workplace relationships in Chapter 3, but how should you improve what you have control over?

When I was a college student at the University of Pennsylvania, I was lucky enough to study with Dr. Martin Seligman, the founder of the positive psychology movement. (I'll tell you more about that class in Chapter 2.) He created something called the PERMA+ model to give people a roadmap for activities that are intrinsically motivating and contribute to well-being and happiness.

The model's five components are:[15]

- **Positive emotion:** These are feelings like hope, joy, compassion, and amusement. You can build these emotions at work by volunteering for activities that you enjoy or sharing pride in your accomplishments (or someone else's).

- **Engagement:** This is like the flow state, when you become so immersed in what you're doing that you lose track of time. One way of doing this is carving out blocks of time for "deep work" that let you flex your skills.

- **Relationships:** Having positive relationships with the people around you is a huge part of being happy at work. Taking the time to get to know some of your coworkers, or agreeing to mentor or sponsor someone, can transform how you feel about your job.

- **Meaning:** Doing work that you feel is meaningful and valuable to others is another big component of job satisfaction. This can mean checking in periodically that what you're doing at work aligns with what you want to be doing, and taking steps to bring those two realities closer together.

- **Accomplishments:** This is also sometimes called achievement, mastery, or competence. Being able to achieve the goals you've set for yourself, and apply the skills you've worked hard

17

to develop, contributes immensely to your well-being at work. And don't forget to celebrate those accomplishments before you move on to the next thing!

The "+" was added later and refers to additional elements of mental well-being like optimism, nutrition, physical activity, and sleep.

Creating a daily habit of making time to work on even one of these components will put you in the driver's seat of your workplace happiness.

Looking Forward to the Happiness, Works Framework

While many people let these myths get in the way of their happiness, not everyone does. I talk to many people who are happy at their job. These conversations are a lot different from the ones earlier in this chapter. Those people who love their work aren't thrown off when things don't go the way they want. They talk more about internal rewards than external ones. As it turns out, they're also often the most successful people in their organization. In fact, it was talking to these people that got me interested in studying workplace happiness in the first place.

What they told me confirmed much of what I instinctively knew. These conversations—and the surveys, the interviews, and other research tools I used to figure out what was happening at these large organizations—led me to think about happiness in a more specific, clear way. And that is what helped me to develop my own five-step framework that combines some of the world's best research on workplace happiness with stories from people who are already doing the right things (and reaping the rewards). That's what I want to share with you in Chapter 2.

Chapter 2

What Is Happiness?

I want to tell you a story.

Let me introduce you to Helen Russell. Her book, *The Year of Living Danishly*, is an amazing story of what it's like to live in one of the world's happiest places.

Helen was living in London, where she was an editor at *Marie Claire*, a fancy fashion magazine. One day (a Wednesday, to be exact), her husband came home and told her that he'd been offered his dream job—working for LEGO. She was excited, until she heard the job was in a place called Billund, Denmark (the birthplace of LEGO), a town of 7,300 people that's a three-hour drive west of Copenhagen in the middle of the Danish countryside.

Now, Helen loved living in London. But she and her friends barely had time to connect. It felt like she and her busy friends never had time to actually enjoy their city.

But Denmark? She barely knew how to find Denmark on a map, let alone set up an entirely new life there. They decided to give it a year. She took a leave of absence from her job (just in case things didn't work out), and shipped all of their stuff across the North Sea.

Now, let me tell you a little bit about Denmark. Because that is integral to this story.

You may have heard of "blue zones," where unusually high numbers of people live long and healthy lives. These five regions, first reported on by *National Geographic* fellow Dan Buettner, have attracted a lot of media attention in the past 20 years. People in blue zones are physically active and have low levels of stress, lots of social interactions, and a balanced diet made up mostly of locally grown whole foods. Not surprisingly, their quality of life is through the roof and disease rates are exceptionally low.[1] Sounds like a pretty good recipe for happiness, doesn't it?

What you might not know is that Buettner has also identified specific "happiness" blue zones. These focus more on places with exceptional levels of happiness, rather than longevity. What's really interesting is that happiness blue zones have different characteristics than longevity blue zones.

While the original blue zones focus a lot on physical things like exercise and diet, the key factors for happiness are more internal. A few of them are:

- **Purpose and meaning:** Purpose is a central part of people's everyday lives, whether that comes from culture, community, or work.

- **Economic security:** Everyone in these places has their basic needs met and people have similar levels of wealth.

- **Access to nature:** Their emotional well-being is enhanced by regular exposure to green spaces, bodies of water, or mountains.

- **Cultural attitudes:** More people in these regions have a positive mindset and the communities tend to focus on collective welfare and contentment.[2]

What both types of blue zones have in common is balanced lifestyles without too much stress and lots and lots of social interactions. And I mean *a lot*. The structure of these societies makes social connection easy and unavoidable. And this focus on friendship, connection, and a strong social life is their secret sauce. People there don't treat friendship as something that happens once work is done—social connection is integrated into their work lives just as much as their non-work time.

So where are these magical places? There are four that come up in the research: Denmark, Singapore, Costa Rica (the only place that's also a longevity blue zone), and Boulder, Colorado.

I got very interested in what we can learn from these places. And more specifically Denmark (because that brings us back to Helen).

When people think of Denmark, it's often for their generous social benefits and laid-back lifestyle. In the last few years it's also become known for a concept called *hygge*. Long a staple of Danish life, hygge means "taking time away from the daily rush to be together with people you care about … to relax and enjoy life's quieter pleasures."[3] Think about unwinding at home with close family or friends, maybe sharing a meal or a treat and comfortably passing the time with no agenda. With the chilly temperatures you often get in Denmark, there's an emphasis on coziness and conviviality.

So how do Danes make the time for all of this community, friendship, and connection?

It helps that they only work about 33 hours a week—which, in America, might feel like it only takes us to about Tuesday afternoon! (Just don't think they're lazy. Denmark is one of the most productive countries in Europe, and slightly ahead of the US in GDP per working hour.[4]) This means that they have a lot more time for social connection.

The Danes love their clubs. The average Danish person is a member of about three clubs. These could be about anything from badminton to bicycling to vegetable gardening. *Everyone* belongs to a club (usually several) and people rush to leave work to get to them. An old joke in Denmark is that when two Danes meet, they shake hands—and when three Danes meet, they form an association.

Club culture helps to keep Danes active and socially connected. It also means that, almost without thinking about it, they default to getting a few hours a day building friendships. This may be the biggest reason why a country that gets seven hours of daylight during the winter (and one measly hour of sunshine, on average) is also one of the happiest places on Earth.

When Helen arrived in Denmark, she was apprehensive. She'd never lived in a small community, and she was worried that it would not be her thing. But, she reasoned, it was true that in London she barely had the time to do the things she loved. Maybe it would be different in Denmark?

When she arrived, she decided the best way to fit in would be to join the expected three clubs. She did this, and it only took her a few months to notice a remarkable change in her happiness. She made friends quickly, astounded at what a short amount of time it took for people with common interests to feel like "her people." She had time for creative pursuits that she found fulfilling in a way that she hadn't had in years. She was sleeping better, laughing more, and her relationship with her husband (who had also joined his own clubs) got even better.

A year passed and they never did move back to the United Kingdom.

You may be asking yourself: All this from joining a few clubs and spending time with a new set of friends? I'm not saying that is the whole story, but there's no question that making friends, and investing in those relationships, is a huge part of happiness.

Okay, So What *Is* Happiness?

I never directly answered the question that gives this chapter its title, and it *is* a little more complicated than spending more time with friends (although that's a huge part of it). If, as we saw in Chapter 1, most of us are doing the wrong things to be happy at work, what are the *right* things?

While working 33 hours a week is blasphemy in the United States, it's still true that if we can make more time—even an hour—for activities that connect us with other people, we're moving in the right direction. And there are several other activities that science has shown to move the needle on our happiness in predictable and dependable ways. By the end of this chapter, you'll have a solid understanding of what those activities are. We'll spend the rest of the book diving into the details on the top proven strategies for improving workplace happiness.

I've spent the last 15 years doing the research on these approaches, to understand how happiness works and what consistently makes people happier. Why have I built my career around this quest? I was lucky enough, early on, to learn that happiness is not a magic trick. It's not about "life hacks" or genetics or wishing for it to happen.

Here's what it is: a sustainable, long-lasting feeling that can be accomplished by building the right habits and practice. It's available to everyone, regardless of your circumstances or disposition. At work, and in life, we all have the ability to become happier.

I first became exposed to the idea that happiness was something you could control as a student at the University of Pennsylvania. I signed up for a course called "Foundations of Positive Psychology" with Dr. Martin Seligman, not knowing that he is a world-renowned expert in the field. What he explained was that happiness was not a destination—there's no treasure map to follow, where you arrive and unlock happiness at the very end of your search. It's more like learning how to use a tool: As you get better and better at using it, the tool delivers happiness more easily and regularly. You know you're making progress because your well-being can be defined and measured.

The way he explained it was so simple and achievable that it really helped me to stop overthinking. It gave me the courage to embrace a more optimistic (but still realistic) viewpoint. By the end of the course, I saw a path forward that made happiness seem achievable and would give me the chance to flourish.

The first step was learning how to define and measure happiness.

The Hierarchy of Happiness

If you've ever taken a first-year psychology course, you've probably come across Maslow's hierarchy of needs. First proposed in 1943 by the psychologist Abraham Maslow (in a paper called "A Theory of Human Motivation"), its key idea is that people progress through stages of needs, from the basic (food, water, and safety) to the beautiful (self-actualization and transcendence), as they climb higher in the pyramid. The theory has had a popular place in our culture for more than 80 years because it captures something about how people progress and develop.

We can use the same model to understand happiness. Like the hierarchy of needs, happiness can be understood as a series of levels (see Figure 2.1). At each level are goals you can work to achieve, which become the building blocks of your happiness foundation. After you master a level you progress to the next, creating a stronger foundation and unlocking deeper and more sustainable feelings of happiness.

It helps to understand these foundational concepts of happiness before we move on to learn the specific actions you can take to increase your happiness at work. Remember that you can apply the principles from the hierarchy of happiness to your life at work and outside of it. It's there to give you a roadmap for what kind of activities you need to pursue—and in what order—to take specific steps toward improving your happiness.

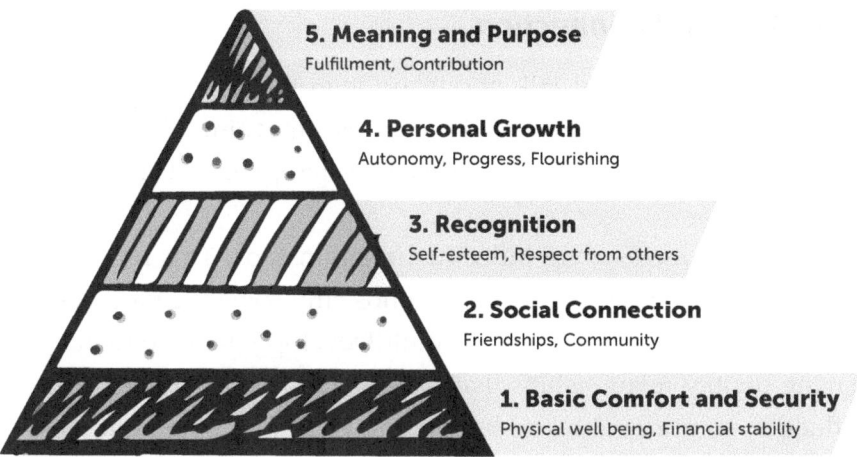

Figure 2.1 The hierarchy of happiness. *Source*: Jessica Weiss.

Level 1: Basic Comfort and Security

Similar to Maslow's hierarchy, this first level acknowledges that you can't be happy if your basic needs are not met. It's difficult to feel secure if you don't have a safe place to live. And it will be hard to focus on your happiness if your health is poor.

I include "financial security" among these basic needs. This doesn't mean that you need a fat investment account and a comfortable retirement secured; it just means that you need enough money to meet your basic needs without constant stress. Savings do help here, in case you have to stop working. Living paycheck to paycheck is stressful because you're always one step away from not having enough. Knowing that you can pay your bills, even if you don't have money coming in for several months (financial planners usually recommend saving enough to cover six months' worth of expenses), prevents a lot of sleepless nights.

While you can still pursue activities at higher levels of the hierarchy, they will have a lot less impact if your foundation level is shaky.

Level 2: Social Connection

There's a reason that I talk about the importance of friendships so often. Human beings are social creatures—meaningful relationships and a sense of belonging are crucial for happiness. This shows up in two ways.

First, we need strong individual relationships. This means regular, daily interactions with family, friends, and romantic partners. Like we saw in the Harvard Study of Adult Development (see Chapter 1), having quality relationships that we are satisfied with is the biggest influence on our health and happiness. They strengthen our feelings of security and reduce feelings of stress.

Second, we need a connection with our community. Feeling like you're part of a group or community helps you to feel accepted and valued. We value "social proof"—if we're accepted by others, it makes it easier for us to accept ourselves.

The strength of our relationships shows up in how we age. As Dr. Robert Waldinger said in his TED Talk about the Harvard study, "Good relationships don't just protect our bodies; they protect our brains."[5] Recent studies of aging populations have found a correlation between the size of a person's hippocampus and the strength of their social networks. Having three or four close and supportive friends can literally delay aging in that region of the brain by a year or more.[6]

Level 3: Esteem and Recognition

For deeper happiness, you need to feel good about yourself. As with social connection, there are two parts of the equation that you have to solve before moving on to the next level.

The first is internal. Developing a strong, steady sense of self-esteem is necessary for happiness. You have to feel like you are *worthy* of happiness before you can achieve it.

The second is external. Independent of our self-esteem, our happiness also depends on being seen positively by others. This usually means being recognized for our contributions and abilities in a way that makes us feel recognized and appreciated.

Interestingly, the importance of internal versus external recognition is influenced by culture. Several studies have found that self-esteem strongly affects happiness in cultures like North America that emphasize the importance of individual values. Respect and recognition from others is more influential in East Asian cultures that emphasize the importance of interpersonal connections.[7]

Level 4: Personal Growth

This level is where your achievement and progress toward your goals deepens your sense of happiness. Having the freedom to make choices, pursue goals, and continually engage in learning and growth gives you a sense of progress that is deeply satisfying for most people. This shows up in a few different ways.

Autonomy helps you feel like you have control over your life and decisions. This makes you more engaged in your work, increases how meaningful it is (because you are responsible for your actions), and allows you to pursue internal motivations (like self-expression).[8]

Being able to pursue and achieve your personal goals increases your sense of well-being because a sense of progress generates positive emotions. It's not just that achieving the goal gives us a dopamine boost, but that the feeling of moving forward itself generates positive emotions.[9]

Growth comes from self-improvement: acquiring new skills and knowledge. Learning new things broadens your perspective, which is correlated with more happiness. It also increases your self-confidence, which a study out of Oxford University found makes you more agreeable and likable. This in turn makes it easier to form positive relationships and get ahead.[10]

Level 5: Meaning and Purpose

At the top of the hierarchy, true happiness involves having a sense of purpose and meaning in life. This could be through work, hobbies, volunteerism, or any activities that feel fulfilling and allow you to contribute to something greater than yourself.

Fulfilling activities are ones that achieve a purpose connected to your "why." So working out and improving your fitness can feel fulfilling if it's contributing to your goal of being healthy into old age so you can spend time with your grandchildren. Or helping your organization achieve a major goal is fulfilling if you really believe in the purpose of that organization.

This goes beyond self-improvement; it's more about helping people or groups that are "bigger than you"—in other words, even more important. Making another person's life tangibly better, or making the world a better place by working for a cause close to your heart, are acts that give your life meaning and help you to write a positive story about your life.

How Do You Know If You're Happy at Work?

It's funny how often people tell me that they're not happy at work, but can't explain why.

Don't get me wrong—they may have a reason (usually something to do with their boss or their organization or their paycheck), but when you drill down, it doesn't hold up to scrutiny. Maybe they were mad at their boss, but they acknowledge that she's really a decent person who's doing her best; maybe the problem isn't how much money they make, but that they haven't progressed as far in their career as they want to.

At this point, I usually ask them three questions that start to uncover deeper issues.

- *Are you having an impact?* As we saw in the hierarchy of happiness, a sense of progress and purpose is crucial for deeper happiness. The feeling that you're moving in the right direction generates positive feelings even if you don't know the impact of your actions yet. When you know you're having an impact, you're often getting recognized for those contributions. Your work has meaning because it is connected to your "why." If you're like me, you want your work to matter and to feel like your contribution is making a difference.

- *Are you working with the right people?* Whom you work closely with is one of the largest environmental factors that affects how happy you are at work. No matter how much you're intrinsically motivated, a coworker who's not pulling their weight, or who brings negative energy into every meeting, is going to bring you down. So if you feel like you're doing the right things but you're still not happy, look around: Are you working with quality people you can trust? Do they bring positivity and energy to your interactions with them? Do they help you learn new skills and inspire you to bring your A-game?

- *Are you growing?* If you're not growing, you will feel as though you're standing still … and the rest of the world is moving ahead. It's easy to see why a lack of growth can make you feel stressed and anxious. On the other hand, a fulfilling job will challenge and inspire you, encouraging you to learn and stretch yourself. Working in a place that promotes innovation and learning makes it easier for you to keep moving forward.

These are all great questions because they're actionable in some way—if your answer is "no" to any of them, you know what you can change to make yourself happier.

For this reason, I think "Are you happy at work?" is actually the wrong question to ask yourself. Instead, think about "When am I *happiest* at work?"

If I'm being realistic, I would probably be happy to answer "yes" to just one or two of my three questions at a particular time. I don't expect all of those things all of the time. So ask yourself: When have I been happiest at work? What was happening? Whom was I working with? What kind of work was I doing? This is a great exercise that will bring more self-awareness and allow you to identify what's important to you.

Everyone wants to find their dream job, but most people imagine it as a position that you just walk into and, like magic, it has everything you want. The truth is that it takes work to bring about those things. Dream jobs don't show up under the Christmas tree; they're something that we create.

The good news is that you get to determine what a dream job means to you. You get to define it. You get to create it.

For some people, it might be making a certain amount of money. For someone else, it's about working in a certain industry, or working with a certain clientele, or making an impact. Maybe it's about getting off at a certain time to pick up your kids from school.

Whatever a dream job means to you, finding it will make you happier at work *and* home. Unfortunately, too many people see this as a binary and let their pursuit of happiness at work detract from being happy with the rest of their life. As the psychotherapist Esther Perel memorably said, "Too many people bring the best of themselves to work and bring the leftovers home."

---

12 Questions to Measure Your Workplace Happiness

Not sure exactly how happy you are at work? It can be a hard thing to measure. Give yourself a rating of 1–5 on each of these questions.

1. Could you recite your company's values without checking?

2. Have you disagreed with your boss in the last month?

---

3. Do you lose track of time at least once a week?

4. Would you trust your colleagues to water your plants?

5. Does your work occasionally keep you up at night (from excitement, not stress)?

6. Have you recently celebrated a coworker's success?

7. Do meetings energize rather than drain you?

8. Could you name three ways your work impacted real people this month?

9. Would you choose your current team if you were starting a company?

10. Does feedback make you curious rather than defensive?

11. Have you broken any "rules" to delight a customer?

12. Do you talk about your work at dinner parties?

If you're scoring below 36, you might be successful, but you're probably not thriving.

What to Do *Before* Pursuing Happiness at Work

As much as I want you to be happy in your career, there are two things that can make it impossible for you to achieve it despite your best efforts. That's why it's crucial that you answer two questions before diving into taking concrete steps toward improving your happiness.

Did You Earn Your Success?

Research shows that success doesn't mean much to you if you don't feel like you earned it. This means that there was fairness and transparency in how you got the job and that you feel like you deserved it.

In the psychological literature, this is known as "attribution theory." Workplace studies assessing the theory found that when employees attribute their success to internal factors (like effort or skill), rather than external factors (like luck or favoritism), they show higher motivation, performance, and job satisfaction.[11]

A 2008 study looked at how these attribution styles affected people's career trajectories. It found that employees who believed their success was earned through merit, rather than luck or connections, showed better relationships with their supervisors, faster career advancement, and higher salary growth.[12]

Are You Doing Work That Others Can't Do for Themselves?

It's important that you feel like your work is helping someone. You need to be doing something for someone else that they could not do without you.

Adam Grant, the #1 *New York Times* bestselling author whose books have sold millions of copies, is perhaps the most famous organizational psychologist in the world. He has done a lot of work that shows how helping others makes you happier *and* better at your job:

- He found that reminding doctors and nurses that handwashing helps patients increased their handwashing by 10 percent and soap use by 45 percent.[13]

- In a different study, he found that when university fundraisers (trying to raise money for scholarships) spoke to the scholarship recipients for five minutes about how receiving that scholarship benefited them, workers spent 142 percent more time on the phone each week and brought in 400 percent more revenue—even a month later.[14]

- In a third study, Grant found that lifeguards who read four stories about other lifeguards saving drowning swimmers worked 43 percent more hours and increased helping behavior by 21 percent.[15]

People often make the mistake of thinking too narrowly about what "help" means. Many of us underestimate the significance of what "help" truly encompasses. The fast-food worker provides more than just a meal—they offer someone a moment of relief from cooking after a long day. A bookkeeper isn't merely processing numbers—they're sustaining the financial framework that keeps an entire organization running and employees paid. Taking time to recognize the ripple effects of your work—how it genuinely improves others' lives—can transform your perspective and cultivate a deeper sense of fulfillment.

How to Be Happy at Work: A Framework

Now that you understand the ingredients of happiness, and the prep work to do before you begin, it's time to unveil the recipe. The framework that I've developed has been built over 15 years of reading the latest psychological research, sharing that research with teams at dozens of organizations, and careful observation and study of people who are happy at work. I've seen firsthand, over and over, how applying these steps has led to happier and more successful teams. Teams that follow this recipe flourish because they work in engaging environments that are powered by lasting and sustainable satisfaction.

Step 1: Making More Friends

Friends are magic. As we saw with Helen Russell's story in Denmark, having a set of dependable friends you can trust can transform how you feel about your environment and your life. It turns out that this basic element of personal happiness also applies to our teams and our organizations. People who feel a sense of belonging with their coworkers show a 56 percent increase in job performance and are much less likely to leave their jobs or take sick days.[16] Teams with deeper, richer social interactions do more innovative work and get more satisfaction from their work.

The challenge is that making friends isn't always easy, especially at work. As we'll see, the majority of us don't have a genuine friend at work. So in Chapter 3 we're going to dive into how to change that.

We'll talk about how to attract your ideal friends and how many you need to change how you feel about your job. We'll leverage phenomena like the exposure effect and the likability gap to make it easier for you to meet and connect with your coworkers, as well as science-backed ways to collaborate that will make you closer to each other *and* more effective.

We'll also look at who are the most important people to develop friendships with (and how to do it), along with insights into what kind of conversations lead to genuine connections.

Step 2: Cultivating Resilience

That old philosopher (and boxing champion) Mike Tyson famously said, "Everyone has a plan until they get punched in the mouth."

For most people, happiness disappears at the first sign of trouble. This makes sustained happiness impossible, so you need to learn how to keep focused on what enhances your well-being and is within your control.

The goal of this book is to make happiness a feeling that persists within you no matter what kind of storm you need to weather. This means looking at the strategies and techniques that will let you and your team develop resilience so you don't get knocked off track (or knocked out). Chapter 4 gets you started.

We'll do this by looking at how the US Army actively trains resilience and what you can learn from them. We'll also dive deep into proven techniques for becoming more resilient at work and real-world examples of how applying these techniques led to improvements and even transformations in different large organizations.

Step 3: Building Trust and Psychological Safety

Trust—in coworkers and organizations—has a profound impact on happiness. The key to building trust is establishing psychological safety, that shared belief within a team that it's okay to take risks and that you can speak up without being punished or humiliated. Studies have shown that it's a crucial ingredient for happy, successful teams. We'll look at what it is and how to know if you have it starting in Chapter 5.

But how do you create an environment where trust will flourish? We all know the feeling of a relationship that is grounded in trust. It's the cornerstone of effective team dynamics. When team members trust each other, they are more willing to collaborate, share ideas openly, and support one another. But the challenge lies in understanding how to earn that trust. What's the game plan for how we can build trust across our team?

We'll look at four practices you can adopt that have been proven to increase trust in almost any organization, along with what a trust-infused environment can unlock for your team (and how this relates to happiness).

We'll also dive into several case studies that demonstrate how teams in different industries have built extraordinary psychological safety—from a counterintuitive practice at a high-end hotel chain to trust-building stories from Ford and Pixar.

Step 4: Weaving Progress and Accomplishment into Each Day

In the hierarchy of happiness, we saw how important a sense of progress is for reaching your higher-level happiness goals.

This is what makes the difference between a good day and a bad one. Or between a good day and a great day. A major driver of day-to-day happiness at work is feeling that you are making progress toward something meaningful. While it's important to have goals, and to work toward those goals, you don't actually have to accomplish them to be happy—you just need to know that you're making progress.

In Chapter 6 we'll look at the science that explains this (the "progress principle") and how to design your days to remove the obstacles to progress. It starts with harnessing the power of purpose—that deep internal motivator that will help you to bulldoze through whatever stands in your way. You can then take that understanding and use it to design your day, getting yourself off autopilot and building momentum by setting up a series of bite-size milestones.

We'll also look at a case study from a large Fortune 500 company, where one simple change took a stalled team and helped it to ride a feeling of progress to stronger collaboration and innovation.

Step 5: Building Practical Optimism into Our Everyday Lives

A large part of making happiness sustainable is embracing a bias toward positivity and optimism. This isn't "blind optimism," or just hoping things will work out, but a strategic practice that helps you lock in a positive mindset, as you see in Chapter 7.

We'll look at the neuroscience research that can help you to rewire your neural pathways for more happiness. We'll then put the research into practice with straightforward habits you can employ that have been proven to inject more happiness into your day.

We'll learn how to use enthusiasm as a tool to rally your team. And we'll learn why incorporating an element of surprise into how you show gratitude will make it more effective.

Finally, we'll look at concrete ways to handle rejection and turn it around to get you over the roadblocks that stop your optimism in its tracks.

Now we've learned the dead-end roads to happiness that we should avoid, how to think about building happiness over time, and, finally, the recipe for becoming happier at work.

That means it's time to get started.

Chapter 3

But How Do You Actually Make Friends at Work?

Ever notice how making friends as an adult feels more complicated than it should be? Science shows something fascinating about how friendships actually form.

Let me share what happened in my yoga class. In my first class, I hugged the back corner—a classic newcomer move, trying to stay invisible while awkwardly twisting into poses. You know what I'm talking about. It's that initial anxiety that you get whenever you walk into a new place filled with strangers.

Week after week, I took the same spot and I saw the same faces around me. Week after week, I'd arrive early to claim "my spot." Soon I noticed others had their territories, too, creating an unspoken map of regulars. Gradually, nods became smiles. Smalltalk about class temperatures evolved into real conversations. Coffee invitations appeared. Within months, our post-yoga brunches became a highlight of my week.

Without trying, I'd built deep friendships through simply showing up in the same space.

Studies from social psychology confirm this pattern: Consistent proximity + shared experience = authentic relationships. Our brains form stronger bonds when we have environmental consistency—especially in vulnerable situations like a brand-new yoga class. The magic isn't in forced networking. It's in showing up, breathing together, and letting connections unfold naturally through shared practice.

Now, I still look forward to my yoga class, but just as much for the social benefits as the physical ones. Within a couple of months, I moved from trying to pick the most invisible spot in the room to having a whole new group of friends. It's really deepened my enjoyment of yoga and it didn't require any tricks or special hacks—I just needed to keep showing up. I just needed to become a regular.

Why Having Friends at Work Matters

Think having friends at work is just a nice bonus? Nothing could be farther from the truth. It's actually a must-have.

Surveys show that having friends at work is one of the top predictors of workplace happiness.[1] When it comes to happiness at work, what really matters is not *what* we work on, but *whom* we work with.

Remember my yoga story—starting in that back corner, trying to stay invisible? Week after week, same spot, same faces. Those small nods became conversations; coffee dates evolved into brunches. Just showing up consistently created real friendships. Building these friendships completely changed how I felt about that yoga class, even though nothing about the class itself actually changed.

The same principles apply at work and the impact is remarkable. Research shows people with close work friends are:

- Twice as satisfied with their jobs
- More innovative and productive
- More likely to engage customers and partners
- Significantly happier overall[2]

And here's the beauty of work friendships. You don't need many. In fact, you only need one. Now let me be clear; this is not a trivial concept. This is about having someone at work you trust and who gives you support, someone to celebrate your wins, and someone to be there for you during the losses. Having friends at work is one of the best things you can do for your happiness.

Yet so few of us believe this. Only 20 percent of us have genuine work friendships. And, not surprisingly, remote work has made this even harder. According to Gallup, having work friends has become even more crucial since the pandemic started.[3]

Why aren't we connecting more? Americans have been getting increasingly isolated for decades. Between longer commutes, increased work hours, and the pull of our phones, we're often too exhausted to invest in relationships. Here's the irony—connection is exactly what fights that exhaustion.

The Costs of Disconnection

If we look at people who report *not* having a close friend at work, the costs of isolation are alarmingly high. Besides being less productive and less attached to your workplace, not having at least one good friend at work leads to:

- Missing more days of work
- Higher levels of stress
- Fewer promotions
- Lower job satisfaction and performance[4]

Many people think they have to choose: invest in work relationships or personal ones. This is a false choice. Like a smart investor diversifies their portfolio, diversifying your friendships makes you

41

more resilient. When one area of life gets challenging, the others help you stay grounded.

Dr. Robert Waldinger, a psychiatrist and the director of the Harvard Study of Adult Development, emphasizes the profound impact of relationships—including friendships at work—on well-being and resilience. His research stems from an 85-plus-year Harvard study that highlights how strong, meaningful relationships are a cornerstone of happiness, health, and longevity.

He particularly calls out workplace friendships and the role that those friendships play in our resiliency. Waldinger underscores that having friends at work fosters a sense of belonging, reduces stress, and increases overall happiness.[5] When employees feel connected to their colleagues, they experience greater job satisfaction and engagement, which boosts mental health. Workplace friendships provide emotional support, especially during challenging times. Knowing you have someone at work to share frustrations, celebrate victories, or simply chat with creates a buffer against burnout and setbacks.

This emotional safety net helps people bounce back more easily from stress or failures. One of the central findings from Waldinger's study is that relationships—whether personal or professional—are essential for thriving, not just surviving.[6] In a work setting, friendships cultivate trust, reduce loneliness, and improve collaboration, all of which contribute to greater resilience. Waldinger notes that when people work toward shared goals or find meaning in their work together, the connection deepens. This sense of shared purpose and camaraderie amplifies both individual and collective resilience.

But here's the good news: Building these connections isn't complicated. It just takes showing up consistently and being open to natural connection.

Connecting Up and Down the Corporate Ladder

We tend to think about connecting with people either at our level (for example, our team) or one rung above (like our manager). But that's leaving a lot of great potential relationships unexplored. Here are two things you can try to get to know people a little further outside your immediate circle.

Ask for a Skip-level Meeting

A skip-level meeting is a meeting with your manager's manager. Why would you want to do this? For starters, that person will probably have good insights on how to work with your manager. They'll also be able to speak to the big-picture issues facing your area of the company and maybe introduce you to some good people to know.

Many people feel awkward asking for a skip-level meeting—they think it will be seen as "going behind the back" of their manager (definitely tell your manager you're having the meeting) or the "skip" won't have any interest in talking to you. In fact, many executives are interested in getting a better understanding of what people "on the front lines" are facing and will appreciate your initiative.

Become a Mentor or Sponsor

If you're a little further along in your career, volunteering to mentor or sponsor someone more junior can be very fulfilling. Mentors are like coaches, sharing knowledge and providing guidance; sponsors are more like advocates, taking an interest in a person's career and actively "opening doors" for them and promoting them for opportunities. In both cases, you'll get to know someone younger whom you likely wouldn't have been close with otherwise, and you'll get satisfaction from helping them in their career.

But How Do You Actually Make Friends at Work?

Sympathy Circle: Your Team

If your manager is your most important relationship at work, then your team is a close second. Research consistently shows that people thrive when they feel supported, valued, and connected.[7] Your immediate peers are going to have a bigger impact on that than anyone else.

MIT's Human Dynamics Lab has really explored the impact of teams. The numbers are startling: Teams with strong social bonds have 50 percent higher communication than teams with weaker bonds. When comparing team performance, MIT found that 35 percent of the variation between teams could be explained by informal social interactions.[8]

Spending time with your teammates, collaborating with them, and getting to know them as people are all pathways to closer connection and satisfaction. As a happy byproduct, these actions will also improve your job performance. Jamie Dimon, the CEO of JPMorgan Chase, says it well: "The best team is not the team with the best players but the team that plays best together."[9]

Active Circle: Your Cross-Functional Relationships

It's easy to focus on the people immediately around us whom we work with every day. But there are a lot of opportunities to build close connections with people one step removed from your day-to-day work:

- People in different job roles whom you're working with on a project
- People in your role on different teams, who do the same work and face similar problems
- Groups who have formed around a shared identity (for example, female managers) or interest (for example, sustainability efforts at your company)

Connecting around a common interest gives relationships a momentum you can build on. Besides bonding over what you have in common, the insights you learn will also likely improve your job performance. Research from Deloitte shows that organizations that use cross-functional teams are more likely to be innovative, adaptable, and responsive, resulting in lower operating costs and higher profits.[10]

The Influence of Gender

Gender plays a surprisingly important role in how we collaborate and connect with our coworkers. Men and women collaborate in different ways and this has a lot of downstream effects.

In general, men are somewhat more likely to collaborate and connect with other men, while women are much more likely to do the same with other women. This can lead to projects and teams that are dominated by one gender—which can be difficult for the minority group, who may speak up less or get passed over for assignments.

Gender imbalances at the leadership level often unconsciously lead to fewer opportunities. For example, if leadership is dominated by men, women may have a harder time finding a female mentor, or creating the relationships necessary to move up into the senior ranks.

On the other hand, research from Northwestern University found that women with a close inner circle of two to three female friends are more likely to land a high-paying executive position than women who lack this network.[11]

The bottom line is that these patterns can hurt collaboration and connection if they're not acknowledged and considered, which reduces your workplace happiness.

How to Make Friends at Work

Think about making new friends—it probably reminds you of being a kid on the first day of school. Everything felt uncertain, and making the "right" friends seemed like it could shape your whole future.

But let's be real: Making friends at work isn't like that. Even when you're new, there are more built-in ways to connect with people. You can't exactly sit in the back and stay invisible. And thankfully, no one's picking teams for dodgeball.

But this is *the* question that I get asked most frequently: How do I actually make more friends at work? What can I do right now that will help me make friends or even improve the friendships that I have at work?

Attract Your Ideal Friends

Here's the thing: Friendship doesn't have to be complicated. A study of 2,000 adults found it takes about 34 hours of time together to go from acquaintance to actual friend.[12] That's roughly one work week with someone you see often.

Still, it can feel tricky, so let's talk about some easy ways to make it happen.

Start with Familiar Faces

Ever notice how you start liking something just because you see it all the time? Psychological research tells us that something really interesting happens with friendships. Known as the mere exposure effect, it basically says that the more often you see someone, the more likely you are to become friends with them.[13]

Making friends isn't about any of the things we assume, like common interests or shared values. It's honestly about how often you see someone. At work, we need to create opportunities for workplace friendships to flourish. We can do this by becoming "regulars" in certain areas of the office or during specific activities. The mere exposure effect tells us that by consistently exposing ourselves to the same colleagues, we increase the likelihood of forming connections.

So become a regular—somewhere, anywhere.

This consistency will lead to a fascinating development. If you take your lunch at the same time every day, or attend the same weekly team meetings, you'll naturally encounter the same faces repeatedly. We're all creatures of habit, after all. Maybe in your office, you have your spot in the conference room, or your spot at lunch—it's in the left-hand corner, front row. After a few weeks, you'll notice that many of your coworkers also have their unspoken spots. You'll start to recognize familiar faces at these meetings, multiple times a week. Gradually, smalltalk will evolve into more meaningful conversations. Coffee catch-ups and team lunches will follow, and soon there will be a whole new group of work friends just because you had your spot.

The mere exposure effect is really magical. Simply seeing the same people on a regular basis will literally increase your liking for one another, making it so much easier to go from acquaintances to friends.

This idea is backed by something called the Allen Curve: Research found that the closer you sit to someone, the more likely you are to talk to them.[14] Desk assignments aren't destiny, though. People are creatures of habit—if you find ways to cross paths with people regularly, familiar faces will soon turn into real connections.

You Need to Talk to More Strangers (But Don't Tell Your Mother That)

Striking up conversations with colleagues can feel awkward, but it doesn't have to be.

Another action that goes hand in hand with being a regular: talking to a stranger. An important step in building workplace friendships is initiating conversations with colleagues you don't yet know well. This doesn't mean randomly approaching people in the elevator or cafeteria. Instead, look for natural opportunities within your work environment. For instance, you might find yourself waiting together for a meeting to start, working side by side on a project, or getting a coffee in the break room. These are perfect moments to make a casual comment about your shared situation in a friendly, relaxed manner.

Here's a secret: Most of us worry too much about how others see us. I think that we all hesitate to start conversations with new coworkers because it feels awkward or we worry about how we'll be perceived. However, there is brilliant research on something called the "likeability gap," which says that we consistently underestimate how positively others view us after interactions.[15] This phenomenon reveals that people typically like us way more than we assume they do.

Understanding that this likeability gap exists can help us totally reframe our approach. Instead of fearing rejection, we can assume that our colleagues are likely to take your friendly comment or question way more positively than you expect. Just knowing that can give you the confidence to initiate more conversations and connections at work.

Okay, let's get specific, because I always love to get into the specifics. A great way to break the ice is by offering a compliment, like on a coworker's presentation skills or their innovative approach to a recent project. This usually leads to an engaging conversation and potentially a new workplace connection. The likeability gap suggests that your colleague will probably appreciate this gesture more than you might anticipate.

To put this into practice, try this exercise with a coworker you don't know well. This approach to talking with strangers will almost always ensure that you're not rejected:

1. Introduce yourself, if needed.

2. Give them a compliment. Research that I just made up right now suggests that if you tell someone that she has a nice dress on, there is a 90 percent chance she'll tell you it has pockets and will share exactly where she got it from.

I'll admit, the thought of initiating conversations with strangers, or making the first move toward a new work friendship, can feel uncomfortable. It kinda makes me cringe a little bit, too. But I know that work friends are incredibly valuable. That's why I always make a conscious effort to foster more connections and friendships whenever I can. And remember, thanks to that likeability gap, your colleague probably enjoyed the interaction even more than you think they did.

Okay, so that's a few specific strategies on starting friendships at work. But workplace connection comes in various shapes and sizes. And it doesn't necessarily mean sitting together at lunch today. Let's talk about connection at work from a different perspective.

Collaboration Is a Shortcut to Connection

Collaboration with teammates is an excellent way to build more connections that lead to friendships (and maybe lunch). The key is working together, meaningfully and in a connected way. This sense of common purpose binds people together, especially when you're all experiencing a sense of progress and accomplishment together.

Having this sense of connection is really important when you're on a team with a diverse set of backgrounds. To connect, people have to feel like they belong in the group. If we don't feel accepted and included, we won't feel connected. That's why rallying a group around a common set of goals or values is so important—if everyone on the team doesn't buy into what the group is doing, that feeling of connectedness won't be there.

Let's look at one legendary and highly collaborative team: the Beatles. It all started with John Lennon and Paul McCartney, who began playing music together as teenagers. I think few people would disagree that their collaboration brought out the best in each other: The duo wrote nearly 200 songs between 1962 and 1970, many of which have endured for more than 50 years.[16]

They worked "eyeball to eyeball," as John Lennon once put it; they recognized and celebrated what each artist individually brought to the table. As Lennon said, McCartney brought "a lightness, an optimism, while I would always go for the sadness."[17] And those songs were then performed by the whole band.

The epitome of collaboration, right? Hmmm, well, we all know how that story ends. Their creative tensions are as legendary as their creative harmony. While the Beatles were certainly the epitome of collaboration, they had as many problems on their team as we all have on our teams.

Their journey is a vivid illustration of the complexities inherent in teamwork. Even amid discord, great teams can achieve extraordinary feats when they harness their collective talents and aspirations. The Beatles' ability to transcend internal dysfunctions and channel their creative energies into timeless classics remains a testament to their enduring impact on the world of music.

So how can you encourage this level of collaboration among your colleagues in your day-to-day work?

Here's some questions to ask yourself:

- Does your team share progress on the process of their work, not just end results?
- Do your teammates respect that some members of the team may think better on their own?
- Is your team comfortable with the discomfort of creative tensions?
- Can your team come together to fuse something distinct?
- Do team members hold each other accountable?

Putting effort into building open, honest collaboration will lead to more connection and even friendship within your team (and hopefully a couple of timeless classics).

When collaboration is built on trust and openness, it not only gets the job done—it creates connections that can turn into genuine friendships.

Use the Power of Your Circles

If you've ever worked in a growing company (or you're a psychology nerd like me), you may have heard of "Dunbar's number." Robin Dunbar is a British anthropologist and evolutionary psychologist and his famous number refers to the maximum number of people that anyone can maintain stable relationships with. What's the number, you ask? It's 150—the research says this is the maximum number of relationships we can maintain at one time.

In a corporate environment, this is usually applied to team size. The thinking is that if your company (or division or department) is larger than 150 people, you can't know or maintain relationships with everyone in that group, so it should be broken into a smaller group to maintain communication and social cohesion. Many companies, like Gore-Tex[18] and Spotify,[19] limit their team size to under 150 people so those teams can work effectively and company culture remains strong.

This research has been validated with very different types of groups, such as military units, hunter-gatherer societies, modern corporations, and online social networks.

What many people don't know about Dunbar's number is that the research has also explored the limits of our closer relationships. That research says we can maintain relationships with:

- 50 close friends or family members (our active or close network)

- 15 intimate friends (sympathy group)

- 5 of our closest people (support clique)[20]

This has big implications for how we think about our workplace relationships and how we think about nurturing them. I call these different types of relationships your "circles" and we're going to look at how to improve your relationships with each of your circles.

Support Circle: Your Manager

A recent survey on mental health, with 3,400 respondents from 10 countries, really caught my attention. The headline was that your manager has the same impact on your mental health as your spouse.[21]

You know, your favorite person in the world? Your manager is just as influential on your mental health. I mean, think about it—if you hate your boss, you are going to be absolutely miserable.

I can't think of anything that more clearly shows how important it is to have a good relationship with your manager. Almost

70 percent of survey respondents said that their manager impacted their mental health, making managers more influential on people's happiness than doctors (51 percent) or therapists (41 percent).

Consequently, just like you actively work on your relationship with your partner, you need to do the same with your manager. This doesn't mean that you should start planning intimate dinners, but you do need regular, structured time for connection. For a lot of people, this takes the form of a weekly one-to-one.

One-to-ones are a huge missed opportunity. Most of the time, there's a couple of minutes of smalltalk and then you dive into giving a report on all of your activities over the past week. Instead, put those updates in an email and turn your one-to-one into a real conversation.

Have Better Conversations

The number-one barrier to having more friends at work that I hear from people is not knowing how to get started. Many people don't know how to get past "smalltalk" and initiate conversations that are meaningful and lead to more connection.

You don't need to become a conversational expert to make friends, but there are a few simple techniques that you can use to connect with people more easily. Pick a couple that resonate with you and try them out the next time you want to turn an acquaintance into a friend.

Be an "Opener"

People known as "openers" are masters at getting others to open up—and they tend to be very popular, too. Research from Dr. Lynn Carol Miller at the University of Southern California suggests that everyone else can learn from them.

Dr. Miller found that "openers" share some personality traits. They're usually self-aware and comfortable around others. They generally like people and are good at understanding other people's perspectives.[22]

But How Do You Actually Make Friends at Work?

You can become a better "opener" by trying these behaviors:

- **Active listening:** Give people your undivided attention when you speak with them.

- **Expressing empathy:** When someone shares their experience with you, don't just think about what you would do in their shoes (which is human nature), but consciously try to imagine how the experience made them feel.

- **Asking good questions:** Go beyond being supportive and ask people open-ended questions about what the subject means to them. Questions like "What was that like for you?" and "How do you feel about that?" invite people to go deeper with what they're sharing and open up to you.

Great openers are people who really enjoy listening to what others are saying and trying to understand what it means. Having someone open up to you also feels good because people are trusting that you'll respond well, which creates a bond between the two of you.

Why Complaining Is a Dead End
(and What to Do Instead)

Ever notice how a good venting session feels momentarily satisfying but leaves you feeling worse later? Turns out, there's solid science behind this phenomenon.

When we complain, our brains are literally rewiring themselves—and not in a good way. Stanford researchers discovered that habitual complaining actually shrinks the hippocampus, the brain region we rely on for problem-solving. It's like we're

---

training our brains to get better at being negative rather than finding solutions![23]

The physical toll is real, too. Our bodies respond to our negative words as genuine threats, triggering stress responses that weaken our immune systems.

Perhaps most frustrating is what psychologists call "cognitive fixation." The more we complain, the more trapped we become in narrow thinking patterns. Ironically, people who vented about problems were less likely to take any constructive action to fix them.

Psychologist Dr. Martin Seligman's research on learned helplessness explains why complaining becomes a cycle—it reinforces a victim mindset that makes us feel increasingly powerless to change our circumstances.

But there is a better approach: transforming complaints into specific requests and actionable insights. This mental pivot doesn't just solve problems—it rewires those neural pathways toward possibility rather than paralysis. Your challenge isn't never to feel frustrated, but to recognize when you're stuck in the complaint loop and deliberately step out of it.

Be Interested, Not Interesting

Lots of people think that being a good conversationalist is all about having amazing stories to tell and witty remarks at the ready. It's not. In fact, being good at conversation often means not saying anything at all.

Huh? People always give me strange looks when I say this, but it's true. What they're forgetting is that a conversation has *two parts*: the part where you're talking, and the part where the other person is

But How Do You Actually Make Friends at Work?

talking. Everyone focuses on the first part and makes the mistake of ignoring the second.

People think that we can't do much about what other people are saying, but that's not entirely true. What people overlook is the importance of being a good listener. Your goal should be to be interested, not interesting.

Asking people questions *makes them feel interesting*. This makes all the difference. Research from Harvard shows that the number of questions you ask someone you just met has a direct effect on how much that person likes you—the more you ask them, the more they like you.[24]

It's not really a new insight. In his timeless classic *How to Win Friends and Influence People*, Dale Carnegie pointed this out back in 1936: "Be a good listener. Ask questions the other person will enjoy answering."

This is called conversational cathexis. What it means is that great conversationalists pick up on the cues that the other person is giving about what they want to talk about.[25] If someone makes an offhand remark about their kids, or mentions that they recently completed a marathon, this is a hint for you to pick up that it's on the person's mind and they want to talk about it. If you follow up with a few good questions, they'll be interested and immediately pleased with the quality of the conversation. It sounds self-serving, but it's really just a way of telling the person that you care and want to know more about them.

The next time you're meeting someone new, and you're wondering where to take the conversation, you have two choices:

- Ask about something they just said.
- Relate what they just said to something about yourself as a way to establish something in common,

You should be doing more of the first than the second, but both lead to an engaging exchange.

It's quite liberating when you realize that the outcome of a conversation rests on the quality of your questions rather than your answers. Instead of mentally rehearsing what you're going to say next as the other person is talking, you're forced to pay closer attention to them. This not only makes you more emotionally intelligent, but sends off all sorts of subtle physical clues—better eye contact and quicker reactions to what they're saying—that enhance social bonding.

Three Conversation Habits That Hinder Human Connection

Connected teams are high-performing teams. Unfortunately, we all have habits that get in the way of deeper connections with each other. Fortunately, each problem has a solution that will keep your team in sync:

1. **Hijacking the conversation.** We all sometimes send signals that say, "I'm going to need you to finish that story real quick so I can tell you how the same thing happened to me." It can feel like an opportunity to share something in common, but it can too easily come off as making the conversation about yourself.

   Instead, share how you felt listening to the person's story—and resist the urge to come back with a story about yourself.

2. **Being a fixer.** It's hard to resist the urge to try and "fix" whatever problem the person you're talking with is describing—we all want to be helpful and look smart. Unfortunately, these "solutions" often get heard as unsolicited advice.

   (continued)

(continued)

The real solution is to ask open questions that give the person the chance to share more details (and feel heard). Then, if you really want to share your solution, ask if they'd like advice before you offer it.

3. **Mental multitasking.** You really want to be a good listener, but there's just so much to do. Before you know it, instead of listening, your mind is off somewhere else, preparing for your next meeting or compiling grocery lists.

It's hard sometimes, but when you find yourself drifting to other topics, make yourself refocus. It helps to listen for what your next question should be. By assigning yourself the "task" of coming up with a question, you'll automatically start listening for clues in the conversation that will help you formulate your question.

A Future Full of Friends

Creating connection in the modern workplace comes from understanding that joy and fulfillment are deeply personal experiences. By creating flexible, supportive environments—that honor individual preferences while fostering meaningful collaboration—we build stronger, happier, and more connected teams naturally.

When organizations prioritize genuine connection and personal fulfillment, they create workplaces where people don't just work—they thrive. This approach leads to more innovative, resilient, and successful teams who find real joy in working together, regardless of their physical location.

Remember: The most successful workplace connections aren't forced or mandated. They grow organically when we create the right conditions for joy, trust, and authentic interaction to flourish.

Stop Talking About Work

To really learn how to pick up a new skill, it often helps to learn from high performers. When it comes to conversational skills, I look at . . . basketball.

Let me explain. One of the top-performing basketball teams of the last two decades is the San Antonio Spurs. Over a 15-year period they won five NBA championships and set a record by winning at least 50 games for 18 straight seasons. They have the highest winning percentage of any active NBA franchise. One of the constants in that run of success is their coach, Gregg Popovich, who also boasts the most wins of any coach in NBA history.

There's no doubt that Popovich is a great tactician and has had some incredible talent at his disposal. But he's also built a team culture that emphasizes connection between teammates to build a strong culture. One of his hallmarks is what he calls "breaking bread together."

The team eats together regularly. Their frequent team dinners usually take place at a restaurant picked out by Popovich (who is a bit of a foodie). Popovich's one rule at those dinners is that basketball talk is forbidden. Instead, conversations focus on the players' lives, their families, and their interests outside of basketball.

Remember, basketball is each player's passion, their favorite thing to talk about since they were kids, and the one thing that unites them all. And they're not allowed to talk about it. Why?

The answer is simple: People feel closer to each other the more they have in common. And if you just talk about basketball all the time, you're not going to spend time finding out what those other things are that you have in common. This is especially important for a team like the Spurs, which featured many international players from diverse backgrounds. These players didn't necessarily share a lot of the common experiences that their teammates did growing up, but by spending time talking about whom and what they cared about outside of basketball, teammates were able to find their common interests and concerns.

The same lesson applies to any workplace. If you only talk to your teammates about work, the relationship will only go so far. Talking about your common issues is a great starting point, but you need to push further if you're going to turn colleagues into real friends.

The Happiness, Works Method: Friendship

- **Be a regular.** Whether it's in the lunch room or the board room, find your "spot" and use the "mere exposure effect" to initiate connections and start to build friendships.

- **Mind the gap.** The next time you hesitate to start a conversation with someone, remember the "likeability gap." People will view you much more positively than you think for taking the initiative and starting a conversation.

- **Connect through collaboration.** Pursue something meaningful together—ideally "eyeball to eyeball"—and your shared journey (and wins) will naturally help you form a stronger bond.

- **Think in circles.** When you're looking at whom to build relationships with, remember your circles. Your tightest circles will have the biggest impact on your happiness, but each circle offers a path to more fulfilling relationships.

- **Ask more questions.** The best way to be a great conversation partner is to listen closely and ask good questions about what you're hearing. Move beyond talking about work to learn what cares and concerns you both have in common.

Chapter 4

Unbreakable
Your Step-by-Step Guide to Building Resilience

I want to share a remarkable story about resilience that changed the way I think about happiness at work.

A little over 15 years ago, the US Army faced a crisis that mirrors what many of us are currently experiencing in the workplace—overwhelming stress, burnout, and mental health challenges. Their solution revolutionized how we think about resilience. Instead of viewing resilience as a personality trait that some people naturally have and others don't, they approached it as a skill that could be taught, practiced, and mastered.

This was a breakthrough moment. Think about it—we don't expect soldiers to be naturally good at marksmanship or strategy. We train these skills. Why should emotional resilience be any different?

The Army recognized that bouncing back from challenges isn't about *waiting* for time to heal or *hoping* people will figure it out on their own. It's about giving people concrete tools and techniques they can use to build their resilience muscles.

Let's dig in. It's 2008. The US Army has a big problem.

The Army had been embroiled in the conflicts in Iraq and Afghanistan since late 2001. Many people had been deployed for multiple tours. And what was shocking was that one in five of those returning soldiers had fallen prey to depression, post-traumatic stress disorder, or suicide.

One of the top generals, George William Casey Jr., decided that the Army needed a new approach. He knew that soldiers had to learn how to cope with the incredible adversity they faced, so they could bounce back stronger. General Casey was the country's top military commander in Iraq for three years and he'd seen firsthand the devastating situations that soldiers were forced to confront in the field. Shortly after he was nominated to be the Army's chief of staff, he spearheaded a preventive program called Comprehensive Soldier Fitness (CSF) to give men and women in the field tools to proactively build resilience.

CSF was a bold new approach to training: To thrive, soldiers needed to be not only physically fit, but psychologically fit. They would be shown how to build up their resilience when faced with trauma, tragedy, and unpredictable threats. The idea for the program came out of a conversation between General Casey and Dr. Martin Seligman—the happiness pioneer who got me hooked on studying happiness. CSF was based on principles developed at the Penn Resilience Program by Dr. Karen Reivich and Dr. Seligman.

Comprehensive Soldier Fitness was rolled out to all 1.1 million members of the US Army, who were each required to undergo nearly 30 hours of training. It's a program that helps US Army members improve their physical and psychological fitness with training exercises, assessments, and the help of resilience experts.

To implement it, the Army needed, well, an army of trainers who could teach the basic principles of resilience to their units. The 10-day course for trainers, known as Master Resilience Training (MRT), has been taken by more than 30,000 soldiers. It focuses on developing six major competencies and 14 distinct skills.[1] These Master Resilience Trainers were trained to help subordinates improve their resilience and their thinking skills.

Looking at the competencies, it's striking how naturally they would fit into the agenda for a corporate leadership retreat.

- **Self-awareness:** This teaches people to identify and use their own strengths, and the strengths of others, to overcome challenges.

- **Self-regulation:** When facing a crisis or conflict, people learn how to focus on what they can control and how to move past the event.

- **Optimism:** How to recognize the positive outcomes of any event, even negative ones.

- **Mental agility:** How to reframe negative energy that can hinder performance.

- **Strength of character:** To understand how leaders can guide followers when faced with a crisis.

- **Connection:** How your social network of friends, family, and colleagues can be your safety net in times of trouble.[2]

The key idea behind the Army's training is that resilience is something you can learn.

It's true. Some people just seem to bounce back from tough times more easily than others—it's like they're born with a built-in resilience. But here's the thing: Most of us can actually learn to deal with life's curveballs a whole lot better by picking up a few key skills and putting them into practice.

When you look at the training course, it's obvious that the Army wants their soldiers to rely on particular mental tactics when faced with stress: The course recommends that soldiers avoid thinking traps, fight counterproductive thoughts, manage energy, and even cultivate gratitude.[3] Catastrophic thinking and negative beliefs are the real enemies within.

What all of these skills have in common is that they leverage what psychologists call "metacognition"—that is, getting people to think about their thinking. Studies have shown that triggering meta-cognition is crucial for helping people to make lasting changes.

The goal of the training is to help soldiers not just survive difficult circumstances, but to thrive and grow from those experiences. As General Casey put it, "There is a perception out there that everyone who goes into combat gets post-traumatic stress.... In fact, science tells us just the opposite: The majority of people who go to combat have post-traumatic growth. They're confronted by something very difficult and they are stronger as a result."[4]

The training has proven itself. One study of 611 resilience-trained Army National Guard soldiers and civilians showed that participants were better able to handle stressful circumstances and they reported fewer behavioral health symptoms.[5] The program was so successful that it was also made available to family members of those who serve, recognizing that it's not just the people in harm's way who experience severe stress.

Resilience training has now spread to other militaries and studies have shown that healthcare workers, first responders, and even high-level athletes can reduce mental health issues by participating in resilience training.[6]

The same principle applies to workplace resilience. We can learn specific skills to handle stress, navigate uncertainty, and emerge stronger from challenges. Just like any other professional skill, resilience can be developed through deliberate practice and the right training.

Why Building Resilience Matters (Even If You're Not in Combat)

Now you might be thinking, "That's a great story, but my daily stress isn't exactly comparable to battlefield conditions."

Here's what's interesting about resilience: While most of us won't face combat-level stress, life has a way of testing all of us. Whether it's a family health crisis, relationship challenges, or that promotion that went to someone else, research shows that virtually all of us will face at least one life-altering event. It's not if, but when.

Think about that for a moment. The question isn't whether we'll face significant challenges—it's how we'll respond when we do. And this is where the science gets interesting.

Research shows our responses to major adversity fall along a spectrum. Some people struggle to recover. Most bounce back to their baseline within a month. But here's the surprising part— some people actually emerge stronger.[7] Not just recovered, but transformed.

While most people try to avoid adversity, having the ability to navigate through it has real benefits. In fact, most people (about 75 percent) report unexpected positive changes from navigating serious stress:

- They find more joy in small moments.
- Their relationships become deeper and more authentic.
- They handle future challenges with more ease.
- They spot opportunities that others miss.
- They can often find deeper meaning in their experiences.[8]

It turns out that resilience, like a muscle, grows through stress. Handling stress with the right techniques makes the difference between growing the muscle or getting injured.

People who grow stronger from adverse experiences are benefiting from what is called post-traumatic growth. Research has shown that people who go beyond recovery, and use those experiences to grow, actually end up *happier* than they were before the traumatic event. Post-traumatic growth is the idea that many of us—instead of being flattened by tragedy—have the ability to bounce back and grow from it. In other words, there is an alternative ending to the story of trauma. And not just for a little while, but for the long-term: The lessons people learn allow them to reach a new plateau.

There are four key factors that that determine whether someone grows from challenges:

- Grit and perseverance (no surprise there)[9]
- A growth mindset, or believing that you can improve[10]
- Self-regulation (manage emotions and behaviors)[11]
- Education and learning resilience skills[12]

Here's what's powerful: These factors create an upward spiral. Each time you navigate a challenge successfully, you build confidence for the next one. Your resilience muscle gets stronger.

In the workplace, this translates directly to happiness and success. Studies show resilience training can boost job satisfaction by 10–30 percent.[13]

Why is that? Resilient employees can:

- Turn setbacks into learning opportunities.
- Build stronger support networks.
- Handle workplace stress more effectively.
- Create more positive team dynamics.

Think of resilience as your psychological immune system. You can't avoid all stress, but you can build your capacity not just to survive it, but actually grow stronger because of it.

The big lesson? That devastating project failure, difficult reorganization, or challenging colleague might be exactly what you need to reach your next level—if you have the right tools to handle it.

How to Become More Resilient at Work

Nelson Mandela has a beautiful quote about resilience: "Do not judge me by my successes; judge me by how many times I fell down and got back up again."[14]

A large part of developing resilience is having the courage to go through adversity and learn how to pick yourself up again. We will grow stronger if we can pull ourselves up when we're down.

So how do we give ourselves the best chance for growth? Fortunately, the research again guides us to a few activities that will give us the tools to prosper.

The Power of Small Choices

Think of resilience like a muscle. You wouldn't start a fitness program by trying to lift the heaviest weights. Instead, you build strength gradually. The same principle applies to psychological resilience, and it starts with something surprisingly simple: the power of micro-decisions.

Decision-making is like any other skill—it improves with practice. Each time you make a quick, confident decision, you're building neural pathways for decisive action. These pathways reduce decision anxiety, increase trust in your judgment, and strengthen your tolerance for uncertainty. And they ultimately build your resilience. Studies show people who practice this kind of decisive action experience less decision anxiety, better stress management, more resiliency, and higher workplace satisfaction.[15]

Let's look at how this works in daily life. Instead of spending 20 minutes agonizing over a restaurant menu, give yourself two minutes to choose. Rather than scrolling endlessly through Netflix, pick the first movie that interests you. When shopping, make decisions promptly rather than researching every possible option.

When you choose the first movie that interests you instead of scrolling endlessly, you're not just saving time, you're building psychological strength. You're teaching yourself that discomfort doesn't equal danger, and that confidence comes from action rather than endless deliberation.

This practice gradually transforms into emotional armor. Maybe that movie you picked wasn't the best possible choice, but you learn that you can stop and just pick another one. Or maybe it was better than you expected and you feel more comfortable taking a risk next time. By using small choices to build your resilience, you develop the strength to face decisions with confidence, knowing that whatever path you choose, you have the ability to handle both its rewards and challenges. You are learning to feel comfortable with change. By regularly practicing decision-making, you are building and reinforcing the neural pathways that reduce decision anxiety.

The workplace offers countless opportunities to practice this skill. That email you've been crafting for hours? Give yourself five minutes to write and send it. Those meetings you're trying to schedule perfectly? Pick a reasonable time and move forward. Each quick decision builds your confidence for bigger choices.

Think of each decisive action as a deposit in your resilience bank account. When major decisions arrive—like taking a new role or navigating organizational change—you have a wealth of confidence to draw from. This translates to more efficient team decisions, better handling of uncertainty, and more confident leadership. The goal isn't to make perfect decisions, but to build the confidence to act despite uncertainty.

Remember, resilience isn't about avoiding discomfort—it's about moving forward despite it. Each small choice builds your capacity for bigger challenges.

Reframe Stress and Negativity

Another key mindset skill is reframing: counteracting the negativity and stress we face so that it doesn't stop us from taking action.

In Chapter 1, we saw that the vast majority of us have a bias toward negativity—it's a survival mechanism that has existed within us for thousands of years. I've been leading creative sessions for nearly that long and every single time I hear a new idea in one of these sessions, my first instinct is always "*Ooh,* that's an awful idea." Yes, I judge the idea.

But I don't let that stop me. Instead, I keep that thought inside and I listen for a different voice in my head—the one that's saying, "Okay, there is a problem with this idea, but how can I make it better?" Then I work with the person who proposed the idea on how to build on it so that it becomes useful.

Doing this has taught me that negativity shouldn't (and can't) be avoided, but you can treat it as a signal that will lead you to positivity.

We can also reframe stress. Stress often gets a bad reputation. But what if stress isn't the villain we make it out to be? What if, instead, it's simply a signal—our mind's way of nudging us to pay attention to something we deeply care about?

We can reframe stress as a signal for courage. Stress is simply a trigger for a cascade of physical and mental responses designed to help us rise to the occasion. In other words, stress isn't inherently bad—it's our interpretation of it that shapes its impact on us.

Research consistently shows that the way we think about stress matters more than the stress itself. When we view stress as a resource rather than a threat, everything shifts. We perform better under pressure, bounce back faster, and even enjoy better health outcomes.[16] This mindset shift is transformative, but it requires conscious effort—because most of us instinctively see stress as harmful.

So how do we reframe it? Start by recognizing stress as a sign that something meaningful is happening. For example, consider the nerves you feel before public speaking. Instead of interpreting that nervous energy as dread, try labeling it as excitement. Studies have found that this simple reframing—saying "I am excited" instead of "I am nervous"—can boost performance by up to 22 percent during tasks like public speaking. It's even been shown to improve karaoke scores by 27 percent![17]

I actually do this. I am nervous before every single speaking opportunity that I have. But I reframe that stress as energy that I can use. It takes training, but it works.

Tennis legend Billie Jean King encapsulated this mindset when she said, "Pressure is a privilege."[18] Stress arises in moments that matter—moments that offer us a chance to grow, succeed, or do something remarkable. By embracing stress as a signal of importance, we can harness its energy and turn it into fuel.

Stanford researchers have found that 86 percent of people improved their job performance when they saw stress as helpful.[19] This reframing isn't just a mental exercise; it's a practical tool for thriving under pressure. Stress, when viewed through the right lens, becomes a powerful ally—a reminder that you're stepping into an opportunity that matters.

Build Your Support System

When you think of Navy SEALs, you probably picture elite warriors, known for their unparalleled toughness and ability to handle the most dangerous missions. And while individual performance is critical, the secret to their success lies in something deeper: their support systems. SEAL teams thrive because of their extraordinary teamwork, built through rigorous training and a culture that emphasizes collaboration and mutual trust.

This wasn't always the case. In earlier years, SEAL training focused almost exclusively on individual mental toughness. Struggle was seen as a personal failure, and recruits were expected to "tough it out" on their own. But over time, this mindset revealed its flaws. The intense isolation of this approach contributed to rising rates of burnout and post-traumatic stress disorder (PTSD).

Leaders realized that resilience wasn't just about the strength of the individual—it was about the strength of the team. So, they overhauled their training programs with a focus on support and shared resilience.[20] Here's what they changed:

1. **Comprehensive post-combat support:** SEALs returning from combat often faced immense challenges transitioning back to civilian life. Programs like BATTLEMIND, developed at Walter Reed Army Institute for Research, provided soldiers with tools to address mental health challenges. These included PTSD checklists, education on recognizing depression, and strategies for managing anger.[21] Research showed that soldiers who received this training reported fewer symptoms of PTSD and depression, as well as improved sleep.[22]

2. **"No blame" debriefings:** Post-mission debriefs became mandatory—and more importantly, they were framed as "no blame" environments. The focus wasn't on pointing fingers but on learning and improving as a team. These open discussions encouraged honesty about challenges faced in the field, and the insights gained were documented and shared to help others prepare for future missions.

3. **Vulnerable, team-oriented leadership:** Leaders were encouraged to model vulnerability and emphasize team success over individual heroics. They normalized the use of mental health resources and supported the creation of peer counseling programs. This cultural shift helped reduce stigma around seeking help and strengthened bonds across teams.

The results were remarkable: Mission success rates improved, PTSD rates declined, and retention rates rose. Teams became more cohesive and effective because their members knew they could rely on one another for support.

While SEALs operate in extreme conditions, these lessons are just as relevant to any workplace or team. Support systems—whether formal structures like training programs or informal ones like trusted colleagues—are the foundation of resilience. They provide the safety net that allows people to recover, grow, and thrive under pressure.

So how do you apply this in your own life or organization? Start by asking yourself:

- Do you have someone you can turn to when things don't go as planned?

- Are your teammates or colleagues able to give you honest, constructive feedback that helps you grow?

- Do you actively seek out diverse perspectives, or are you surrounded by people who only tell you what you want to hear?

Building support systems isn't just about handling challenges—it's about preparing for them. When you create an environment where people feel safe to share, learn, and support each other, you build a team that's not only resilient but capable of thriving in the face of adversity.

Resilience isn't just about individual grit. It's about the strength of the connections around you. The tighter and more supportive those connections are, the stronger the team—and the individuals within it—become.

You're More Than Your Work, Right?

Just like an investor benefits from diversifying the stocks in their portfolio, we benefit from having more than one source of meaning and purpose. Putting all of your eggs in the work basket is a very perilous proposition. The stock market goes through "crashes" once or twice a decade, and there will inevitably be moments of crisis in your career, too. When you diversify your identity beyond your work, it gives you a more stable and resilient foundation to rely on when things get tough.

People who've invested in different facets of their being tend to be more resilient when adversity arrives. This just makes sense. Having hobbies and outside interests tends to make people more innovative. They can find inspiration from other parts of their life and use it to creatively solve problems at work.

As we saw with the happiness hierarchy in Chapter 2, meaning and purpose play a crucial role in our happiness. Even a fulfilling job can't satisfy all of our needs. Having diverse sources of meaning outside of your job gives you more strengths to draw on when you need them, making it easier for you to feel consistent happiness.

Help Others to Recharge Yourself

When we think about self-care, we often picture moments of solitude—resting on the couch, taking a long bath, or indulging in something just for ourselves. But what if one of the most effective ways to care for yourself is to shift your focus outward, to do something meaningful for someone else?

Helping others is more than just a kind gesture—it's a profound way to boost your own well-being. Acts of generosity have been shown to lower stress, increase happiness, and even improve physical health.[23] The act of giving doesn't just help the recipient; it also lights up areas in the brain associated with reward and pleasure. In fact, research has found that helping others activates the same neural pathways as enjoying your favorite meal or listening to a beautiful piece of music.[24] This is what psychologists call the "helper's high," and it's one of the reasons why giving feels so good.

Beyond that immediate boost of happiness, helping others can also have long-term benefits. By offering your support, you strengthen your social bonds—the very connections that become your safety net when times get tough. Studies have shown that people with strong social ties are more resilient, better equipped to handle adversity, and report higher levels of life satisfaction.[25]

What's remarkable about this approach is how it works to recharge you in ways that passive rest simply can't. When we're burned out or overwhelmed, the temptation is to retreat—to isolate ourselves, binge a favorite show, or simply do nothing. While rest is undoubtedly important, there's a different kind of energy that comes from engaging with others in a meaningful way. Helping someone else shifts your focus away from your own stressors, offering a mental reprieve from the cycle of worry and rumination. At the same time, it provides a renewed sense of purpose, a reminder that your actions matter, and that you're capable of making a difference.

Take, for instance, the simple act of offering support to a friend. Imagine a colleague is struggling with a project, and you step in to lend your expertise or even just a listening ear. Their gratitude not only strengthens your relationship but also leaves you with a sense of accomplishment and connection. Or consider volunteering your time for a cause you care about—helping at a local shelter or mentoring someone in your community. Studies have shown that people who volunteer regularly experience better mental health and even live longer.[26]

Even small, seemingly insignificant acts can have a big impact. Think about the last time you bought someone a coffee just because, or complimented a coworker on a job well done. Those moments may have felt small in the moment, but their ripple effects—on both the recipient and yourself—are anything but. These acts of kindness, however modest, remind us of the joy of human connection and help us step outside our own bubble of stress.

And it doesn't stop there. This outward focus often creates a feedback loop. The more you help, the more others want to reciprocate, building a culture of mutual support. The more you energize others, the more energy *you* have—because "energy is infectious."

When you care for others, you care for yourself in return. It's a different kind of recharge—not just about physical rest but about filling your emotional reserves with purpose, connection, and joy. So the next time you're feeling depleted, try looking outward. Call a friend to check in, offer help to a colleague, or find a cause that inspires you. You might be surprised by how quickly you feel reenergized and more capable of taking on the challenges ahead.

In the end, self-care isn't just about what you do for yourself—it's also about what you do for others. And in helping others, you may just find that you're helping yourself in the most meaningful way possible.

Not All Batteries Charge the Same Way

It's important to recognize that people recharge in different ways. Extroverts are energized by spending time with other people, so they might recharge by having a coffee in the lunch room and chatting with several coworkers. Introverts, on the other hand, need to get away from others to recharge. A one-on-one conversation with a friend might do the trick, but they may also need to find a quiet place to be alone with their thoughts before reengaging with others.

Use PTO to Avoid Burnout

According to the US Travel Association, 55 percent of Americans are not using all of their paid time off.[27]

Similarly, according to a recent survey from Aflac Insurance, 59 percent of Americans experience at least moderate levels of burnout (including 71 percent of Gen Z).[28]

Do you think there's a connection?

Once again, we too easily let work encroach on the time we should be using to recharge and invest in our relationships. Even when we do take time off, we're not able to fully disconnect from work—in fact, more than half of us report that we *continue to work* in some capacity during paid time off.[29]

This is a recipe for burnout. When we don't take time off, life inevitably catches up with us. Just looking at the benefits of a vacation (or even a "staycation") tells us what we're missing out on:

- **Rest:** Taking time off allows us to reduce the "sleep debt" that most of us have and reset our sleep patterns. Research done by the American Psychological Association shows that an extra

60–90 minutes of sleep can improve both memory and concentration.[30] And you don't need a study to tell you that getting more sleep will make you less irritable, anxious, and annoyed.

- **Reduced stress:** We spend many of our busy days with elevated levels of cortisol. Chronic elevated stress hormones depress your immune system, making you more likely to get sick. In fact, a study of 749 women from Massachusetts found that women who took a vacation only every six years were nearly eight times more likely to develop heart problems than women who vacationed twice a year.[31]

- **Time to dream:** A lot of us simply lack the time to take a step back and think. Time off helps us do this by injecting unscheduled time into your day where you don't have an immediate responsibility to fulfill. Just decluttering your mind for a few days gives space for new ideas to fill the space. This is how people often get their best ideas when they least expect them—because they've created time and space for them to appear.

While these benefits might sound like "nice to haves," taking time off has been shown to improve your job performance and recognition. One study from Ernst & Young found that, for every 10 hours of vacation time an employee took, their job performance improved by 8 percent. Those who took vacations more frequently were also less likely to leave the firm. Other research has shown that taking all of your allotted time off actually *increases* your chances of getting a promotion or a raise.[32]

Overlooking the importance of recharging and self-care may be standing in the way of doing your best work. As the writer Anne Lamott put it so beautifully, "Almost everything will work again if you unplug it for a few minutes, including you."[33]

Don't Wait Till Things Are Bad: Practice Boosting Your Resilience

Self-care is prevention, not medicine. You should be engaging in it regularly, rather than using it to treat yourself *after* things have already gone wrong.

How do you do this? Scheduling time to recharge and get away is important, but you can also boost your resilience with practices that have been shown to improve mental well-being. One of my favorites is called "The Joy Journal."

Here's how it works. All you need is five minutes at the end of your workday:

1. **Write down three "successes" from the day.** They could be big ("reached our OKR for the quarter!") or small ("I got a reply to my cold email"), but they have to involve your work. Try to think of something that made you proud or happy.

2. **Note your contribution to each success.** How did you make this event happen? Was it something you do all the time or did you try something different? Is it repeatable?

3. **Identify what enabled success.** Why did what you were trying to do work? Can you learn from that? Can you apply it to another part of your life?

The trick is to make the practice a habit and try to do it every day to increase happiness and well-being. If you can keep it up for a week, you'll probably notice an impact. In one study, 94 percent of severely depressed patients who followed this practice for 15 days improved to experiencing only moderate or even mild depression.[34]

The same strategy can be used to build team happiness. Here are a few things you can do to give everyone on your team a boost:

- Start your team meeting by asking people to share "quick wins" that have happened since the last time you met.
- Create a "celebration board" where everyone can post (and see) stories of success.
- Schedule monthly "success story sessions" where people can share success stories and the team can do a post-mortem on what led to that success, finding lessons that everyone can benefit from.

In both cases, taking the time to notice (and learn from) success will make you happier and help you see how thorny challenges can be overcome.

Make a Habit of Continuous Learning

People understand that investing in self-care makes you more resilient, but they're often surprised when I say that learning works the same way. But it's true: Spending time learning—as often as you can—makes you more resilient in surprising ways.

Let's look at an example. I think most people are familiar with the feeling of being "stuck" at work. You feel like you're spinning your wheels and not making any progress—you're trapped in a Groundhog Day spin cycle of doing the same thing over and over. Well, the best antidote to that is to learn something new. Take a class, learn a new skill, try working on a different team—anything that stretches you and gets you out of autopilot. Snapping out of autopilot will quickly get you unstuck and stop you from feeling burned out (which is usually what happens when you feel stuck for too long).

If you're learning all the time, you've basically vaccinated yourself against burnout.

That's just the beginning. Dedicating regular time to learning also arms you with new skills that build up your resilience (and probably make you better at your job). It doesn't matter too much what skills you pick up—researchers find that the act of learning itself helps you become more adaptable and more likely to bounce back when you face adversity. Learning increases:

1. **Cognitive flexibility:** Learning makes you more mentally adaptable when faced with new situations. This flexibility has a measurable effect on your resilience and ability to recover from setbacks.[35]

2. **Neuroplasticity:** Cognitive flexibility shows up in studies of new neural connections. Continuous learning makes the brain reorganize itself as it has new experiences, which also boosts our memory and resilience.[36]

3. **Positive emotions:** Learning feels good, increasing feelings of accomplishment and curiosity. It helps you have a positive mindset and that optimism makes you work harder to find solutions to problems.[37]

4. **Self-belief:** You become more confident that you'll overcome difficulties and ultimately succeed. Approaching challenges with more confidence and determination enhances your chances of success.[38]

5. **Coping abilities:** Learning can expand your toolkit of coping strategies and problem-solving skills, which makes you better at navigating and solving difficult situations.[39]

None of this is news to Satya Nadella. The CEO of Microsoft made continuous learning a central part of his turnaround strategy when he took over running the company in 2014. At the time, Microsoft was known for its competitive, but siloed, culture. Employees felt they had to prove they were the smartest in the room, leading to what Nadella called a "know-it-all" culture that stifled innovation and collaboration.

One of Nadella's first acts was to preach a shift to a "learn-it-all" culture. He knew that in the fast-changing world of technology, success would come from communication and collaboration—no one person had all the answers.

In one of his first meetings as CEO, Nadella shared a personal story about a failed project, setting the tone that it was safe to discuss mistakes. This led to a cascade effect where teams began openly discussing challenges instead of hiding them, leading to faster problem-solving and innovation.

Nadella kicked off a cultural transformation built around continuous learning. Company leaders began emphasizing the importance of a growth mindset that encouraged experimentation and learning from failure. Peer support groups and mentoring networks were established. The company even introduced quarterly "learning days" where employees were encouraged to put aside their daily tasks and focus on learning new skills.[40]

Leadership bought into this change in approach, adopting a "model, coach, care" framework that aims to build an environment where employees trust each other and feel like their well-being and growth is being supported.[41] Performance reviews were updated to emphasize learning and helping others.

If you're wondering if these changes paid off, just look at Microsoft's stock price—it's gone up 1,000 percent since 2014. Employee engagement scores have also gone up significantly during that time, and Microsoft—which was struggling when Nadella took over—is once again positioned as an industry leader.

Building a Resilient Happiness

I mentioned earlier that happiness is not a fleeting feeling. Building resilience is the tool you need to make that feeling last and become sustainable. While many people believe that resilience is something that you either have or you don't, it's clear that the trait can (and should) be learned over time. It will not only make you happier, but it will also ensure that you're *unhappy* less often and for less time.

Our workplaces play a key role in developing this skill. As we saw with Microsoft and the US Army, taking the time to teach people in your organization how to become more resilient pays incredible dividends. Becoming more resilient is not a journey that you need to take alone, but one that accomplishes more when taken together.

Whether it's by building more support systems or making continuous learning part of your company culture, fostering trust plays a major role in building resilience. In Chapter 5, we'll talk about how to create that trust throughout your organization.

The Happiness, Works Method: Resilience

- **Practice making micro-decisions.** Getting comfortable with making decisions quickly will build this useful muscle so that you won't hesitate when faced with bigger challenges.

- **Reframe stress.** It's our mindset that determines the impact of stress. By reframing anxiety as excitement, we can increase our performance when stressed and even learn to welcome it.

- **Create your support network.** Whom do you turn to for advice and support when faced with a challenge? You want a team that will offer constructive feedback and diverse opinions to help you navigate any challenge.

- **Make time to help others.** Most of us believe that recharging means "getting away from it all." Doing something meaningful for someone else is just as effective and packs both long- and short-term benefits.

- **Incorporate learning into your workday.** Learning gives you the skills and confidence to take on any challenge. Teams should strive for an environment where gaining knowledge is encouraged, failure is framed as a learning opportunity, and people are proactive about adapting to changing situations.

Chapter 5

Trust and Happiness
An Unbeatable Team Formula

Step into the morning meeting at any Four Seasons hotel. It's 8:30 a.m., and department heads gather in a well-lit conference room, coffee cups and notebooks in hand. The general manager stands at the front, ready to lead what they call the "daily review"—a meeting that will set the tone for exceptional service over the next 24 hours.

The guest relations manager opens her laptop and begins: "Today we're welcoming back Mr. Chen, his fourth stay with us. He prefers the corner suite and only sparkling water in his minibar. Mrs. Rodriguez arrives for her first stay—she noted a severe nut allergy. We've already alerted all restaurants." Heads nod, notes are taken.

Then comes the crucial moment: the Glitch Report. The room shifts slightly as the food and beverage director speaks up: "Last night at 8 p.m., we mixed up two tables' orders in the main restaurant. Table 12 received Table 14's appetizers." He doesn't hesitate or sugarcoat. He details exactly what went wrong, why it happened, and most importantly, how they made it right—comping both tables' appetizers and sending over special desserts.

Around the table it goes. Housekeeping shares a delayed turn-down service. Engineering reports a slow response to a heating issue. Each admission comes with a clear plan for prevention and resolution. No blame, no shame—just honest assessment and problem-solving.

This is what CEO Isadore Sharpe means when he says, "What's important with a glitch is not the error, it's the recovery."[1] In this room, mistakes transform into opportunities. A missed room cleaning becomes a chance to surprise a guest with an elaborate evening turndown complete with extra amenities. A delayed breakfast order turns into a personalized meal with the chef's special attention.

Here's how it works: Every department participates, sharing each mistake that happened on their watch the day before. Each department reports what went wrong and what steps have already been taken to address the glitch. Every hotel department knows what happened and which guest was affected.

The power of the Glitch Report lies in what happens after each admission. Teams collaborate across departments to make things right. The concierge might suggest sending local artisanal chocolates to apologize for a noisy air conditioner. The spa director offers a complimentary massage to make up for a delayed check-in.

Here's how this transparency ripples through the organization: Watch what happens when a new front desk agent, Meghan, admits to mishandling a guest's wake-up call. Instead of fear or criticism, she receives immediate support. The room service manager suggests sending up a complimentary breakfast. The concierge offers priority restaurant reservations. Within minutes, a potential service failure transforms into a chance to demonstrate the hotel's commitment to recovery.

This daily practice shapes the entire culture. In most organizations, people hide mistakes, fearing consequences. But at the Four Seasons, they've discovered something powerful: When you make it safe to admit errors, you create an environment where problems get solved faster and service actually improves.

The Glitch Report does more than solve immediate problems—it builds institutional memory. When a similar situation arises three months later, someone remembers the solution that worked before. Teams learn not just from their own mistakes, but from every department's experiences.

The Glitch Report is an amazing tool for building trust. Let's dig into why it works so well:

- **Transparency:** The Glitch Report system makes it easy for employees to openly report issues or mistakes without fear of reprisal.

- **A focus on learning and improvement:** The purpose of the report is not to assign blame, but to learn from mistakes and improve processes.

- **Inclusive participation:** All employees, regardless of their position, are encouraged to contribute to the Glitch Report. This inclusivity helps build a culture of mutual respect and trust, where everyone's input is valued.

- **Timely and constructive feedback:** Issues reported in the Glitch Report are addressed promptly and constructively. This timely response tells employees that their concerns are taken seriously and that the organization is committed to resolving issues.

- **Positive reinforcement:** By addressing glitches constructively, the Four Seasons supports positive behaviors and encourages employees to continue reporting issues. This positive reinforcement fuels a culture of trust.

This is what true psychological safety looks like in action.

Psychological safety is when team members feel safe to express their thoughts and take risks without worrying about negative consequences. When teams feel safe, it encourages innovation and creativity and friendship. Safer teams embrace trust and collaboration, and they genuinely enjoy working together. They aim for constant improvement and they're more successful. They are happier teams.

But what's the process? What do you have to do to build psychological safety in your teams?

The bottom line is this: Work collaboratively and build trust. But of course, learning how to do this doesn't happen overnight.

The Four Seasons has given us a great example of trust in action. But let's take a step back and look at why trust is so important for workplace happiness.

Building Trust: Your Team's Secret Weapon

We all know what a relationship that's grounded in trust feels like. Think about your closest friend—you can tell them anything, be completely yourself, know they've got your back. That's trust. But here's the interesting part—building that same trust in a team is a whole different game.

Team trust is more complex, but it's also the cornerstone of effective team dynamics. It's the "social glue" that holds teams together. Studying teams that have it is like watching a different sport entirely.

It's only when there's strong trust within a team that we see questions flow freely. In most meetings, people bite their tongues, worried about looking stupid or causing trouble.

But in high-trust teams? People ask the hard questions everyone's thinking but are afraid to ask. "Hey, are we sure this strategy makes sense?" becomes a normal part of conversation, not a career risk.

Communication transforms, too. We've all stared at an email wondering, "Wait, are they mad at me?" In low-trust environments, we assume the worst. But when trust runs high, that vague message from your colleague? You assume they're trying to help, not criticize.

Trust makes teams faster, more efficient, and more productive. When you trust your teammates, you don't waste time second-guessing every decision. Ideas flow quicker, innovation happens naturally, and risks feel less scary because you know your team has your back.

And perhaps the best part? Work becomes genuinely satisfying. Instead of feeling like you're alone, you're part of a team that celebrates wins together, learns from mistakes together, and actually enjoys showing up every day.

To achieve this, you need to understand how trust is created.

The Building Blocks of Trust

Trust is a relationship skill. Before people will trust you, you have to show them that you can be trusted.

So how do you do that? Trust comes down to two essential traits: capability and character.[2] If you can show your team that you have the ability to do good work, and the character to align your work with the rest of your team, trust will bloom.

We're all capable (or else we wouldn't have our jobs), but there are a couple of traits that people look for when they're deciding how capable we are.

- **Competence:** People need to believe that we have the skills, knowledge, and ability to deliver good work. So showing our skills is a way to build trust—whether that's a great presentation, mentoring someone, or even sharing an interesting article from your field with the rest of your team. Showing that we want to learn new skills (and become more competent) also builds trust.

- **Reliability:** You won't build trust if your team doesn't believe that you'll demonstrate your competence consistently. They need to know that you'll show up when they need you. That you will do what you say you are going to do.

Reliability is closely tied to the second building block of trust: character. People with character can be depended on because they have:

- **Integrity:** Your words are aligned with your actions. If you say you'll do something, it means you're going to do it. You're transparent and you take responsibility for your mistakes. You give credit where it's due, rather than try and hog the spotlight.

- **Empathy:** This is how you understand the people around you. So if you're a capable person who does what you're asked to do, that will earn you a fair amount of trust. But if you do all that *and* you offer help to people before you're asked, people's trust in you will go through the roof.

Leadership and the Trustworthy Team

So getting people to trust you is a strong starting point. But successful teams aren't built around one person—you need everyone to be trusting each other. How do you make that happen?

Every team leader should be focused on helping their people trust each other more. It starts with giving them the opportunity to prove their competence and character to each other. Leaders can:

- **Set up structured interactions.** Get people to work in pairs to solve a tough problem. Design your teams for cross-functional work, so that each person can use their strengths to help the other.

- **Encourage social connection.** Building connections is about time and opportunity, not networking and awkward mixers. Send people out of the office together to meet a client or set up your team's seating plan so that it's easy for people to chat throughout the day. (Remember the Allen Curve from Chapter 3? The closer you sit to someone, the more you talk to them.)

- **Help people share their skills.** Have your more experienced team members actively mentor the newbies. Encourage people to share their knowledge with the rest of the team to increase everyone's competence.

- **Recognize the people who are building trust.** Feedback is a powerful tool for managers. When you see people doing things that build trust, recognize it and encourage them to keep doing those things.

You can get individuals to trust each other, but getting your whole team to build trust together takes things to the next level. When the team makes exhibiting trust a habit, and it feels like everyone is pulling in the same direction, trust will skyrocket because you're not just working with one person at a time.

Let me share a concrete example from basketball. The 2014 San Antonio Spurs team that won the NBA championship is often cited as one of the best examples of total team trust in sports. Coach Gregg Popovich instituted what became known as "the beautiful game"—a style of play based on constant ball movement, cutting, and trusting that your teammate would make the right play.

At first, this required individual acts of trust: a player giving up a good shot to pass to a teammate for a great shot. But as the season progressed, a transformation happened. The entire team began to operate as a single unit. Players would make passes before their teammates even cut, knowing they would be there. They averaged the most passes per possession in the league. The ball would zip around the court with 4–5 quick passes until they found the perfect shot.

When players saw their teammates consistently making the extra pass and supporting each other, it motivated them to do the same. The bench players felt just as trusted as the starters. By the NBA Finals, they were playing at such a high level of collective trust that they demolished the Miami Heat's more individual-focused strategy in five games.

This example shows how moving from individual trust to group trust creates compound benefits. Once the whole team bought in and made trustful play their default mode, it elevated everyone's game beyond what any collection of one-on-one trust relationships could achieve.

Team leaders can help their team create trust together in a lot of ways. Nothing builds trust like people demonstrating their competence and character when everyone is together—everybody sees it. As a manager, you can encourage people to show trust by:

- **Getting specific about daily habits:** Making it clear that you value behaviors like punctuality, follow-through, and proactive communication will make reliability into a team value.

- **Using meetings to amplify trust:** Setting rules like "no interruptions" (so everyone is heard) and ending every meeting with a summary of the action items (so it's clear what everyone will do) helps people show empathy and integrity.

- **Being transparent:** Sharing information and always giving the reasons behind a request show people that you trust them to understand your intentions.

- **Helping people learn from mistakes:** As we'll see a little later in this chapter, groups that can speak with candor to help each other avoid mistakes have a huge advantage in building psychological safety.

When Trust Unravels: Prevention and Recovery

Trust is like a delicate tapestry—it takes patience to weave but can quickly come undone if certain threads are pulled. In any team, watch for these subtle but destructive patterns that can fray the fabric of trust:

- **Taking credit for others' work:** If you see this, you need to reassign credit publicly so that the person affected doesn't feel cheated. You can discourage taking inappropriate credit by rewarding people for team accomplishments, rather than individual ones.

- **Information hoarding:** Not sharing information transparently makes people feel that someone doesn't trust them or is trying to gain an advantage. Make it clear that transparency is a team value.

- **Broken promises:** Breaking a promise is an integrity killer. It's going to happen occasionally, but you can repair your integrity by letting people know how you'll fix the mistake (and following through).

- **Favoritism:** Nothing undermines team trust like the perception that there isn't a level playing field. Try to audit how you hand out assignments and praise to make sure you're doing it fairly.

- **Behind-the-back conversations:** People quickly lose trust if they don't feel like you're being honest with them. Have the courage to give candid feedback, rather than tiptoeing around the problem.

Rebuilding Broken Trust: Understanding and Reversing the Downward Spiral

When trust fractures in a team, you need to fix it quickly. Your first task is to diagnose the depth of the damage. Like a doctor assessing an injury, you need to understand the severity before you can treat it effectively. Trust typically erodes through three distinct phases, each requiring its own approach to repair.[3]

To understand how the cycle works, I'll share the story of Sarah, a client of mine who learned the hard way how trust can be broken (and rebuilt).

Phase 1: Defensiveness (The Early Warning Signal)

It's fascinating how trust breaks down. First come the subtle shifts—team members who used to dive into challenges start carefully covering their tracks. You'll see increased self-justification, blame-shifting, and protective behaviors from your team. The good news is that this stage actually presents an opportunity—people are still invested enough to push back and engage in conflict, showing they still care about outcomes.

Sarah first noticed something was wrong when she watched Julian, one of her most confident developers, begin prefacing every decision with "As discussed in our meeting on . . ." At first she didn't think anything of it, but after it happened a few times she realized he wasn't being thorough—he was building a paper trail. Sarah should have taken him aside to see what was wrong at that point, but she was buried in her own deadlines and forgot about it.

Within a couple of weeks, she noticed that the behavior had spread—her whole team was documenting every conversation. Each email had five people CC'd, and people were taking detailed notes in meetings they used to breeze through. The irony? This defensive behavior showed that they still cared enough to protect themselves. There was still time to fix things, but Sarah wasn't sure what to do.

Phase 2: Disengagement (The Quiet Retreat)

If defensiveness isn't addressed, it evolves into disengagement. This isn't just having an off day; it's a pattern of low effort and emotional withdrawal.

Sarah got really worried when she saw her team's effort level begin to drop. Pierre's laptop closed during brainstorming sessions—he used to be her idea generator. Maria used to stay late to perfect projects, but she began leaving precisely at 5:00 p.m. Then one of Sarah's colleagues told her something that really scared her—three of her team members were quietly talking about freelance work they had taken on. They weren't just checking out mentally—they were building escape routes.

Phase 3: Disenchantment (The Point of No Return)

The final stage is when employees emotionally exit the organization while still on payroll. This is when things have gone toxic. More dangerously, they often become actively negative influences, attempting to draw others into their disillusionment. This can lead to mass departures and severe organizational trust issues.

Sarah knew she was in trouble when she overheard Alex in the break room: "Why bother bringing this up? Nothing ever changes here anyway." He wasn't just frustrated; he had become actively cynical and, worse, he was spreading that cynicism. When Jenny, her newest hire, started echoing his attitudes two weeks later, she came to see me.

Breaking the Cycle

Trust fractures have origin stories. When I finally sat down with Sarah, we started with looking back at what might have caused the rupture. I discovered the defensive behaviors started after she dismissed a project recommendation from Julian without discussion. When she finally spoke with him, she discovered that he'd been feeling unappreciated for a couple of months, and that small slight was the straw that broke the camel's back. That broken moment of trust, and the damage it had done to their relationship, had created a ripple effect through the entire team.

Broken trust, it turns out, moves like a virus. Once Julian's defensive behavior became visible, others started questioning their own security. Soon she had a team full of people building individual fortresses instead of bridges.

The Rebuild

We had to go back to basics. Sarah went to Julian and apologized for her behavior, then expressed her desire to reset their relationship. She also spoke to her team about how she felt and how important it was to her to earn their trust again. She added some new weekly trust-building activities (see the nearby sidebar "Five Trust-Building Activities") to their meeting agenda. Finally, she implemented a new feedback system where people could report problems anonymously. And she vowed to start addressing problems when she discovered them, instead of hoping they'd resolve themselves.

While I've condensed this story, the truth is that teams don't lose trust in one dramatic moment. It erodes through a series of small betrayals, each one seemingly too minor to address. But if you can spot that first defensive behavior—that first moment when someone starts protecting themselves instead of contributing freely—you've found your moment to intervene. Fix the crack before the whole foundation crumbles.

The best part? When your team sees you actively working to rebuild trust—not just talking about it, but making real changes—they'll often surprise you with their willingness to rebuild. After all, most people want to trust their colleagues. They're just waiting for evidence that it's safe to do so again.

This brings us to a critical element of high-performing teams: the ability to take risks without fear of punishment or humiliation. Psychological safety isn't just about feeling comfortable; it's about creating an environment where innovation thrives because people aren't afraid to speak up, experiment, and yes, sometimes fail. When team members know that their mistakes won't be held against them—that they'll be treated as learning opportunities rather than career-limiting moves—they bring their full selves to work. They share those half-formed ideas that often lead to breakthroughs. They point out potential problems before they become crises. In other words, psychological safety turns trust from a foundation into a launching pad.

Five Trust-Building Activities

Not sure of the best way to build trust at your team meetings? Try out these five exercises and see how your team trust grows.

1. **The expectations exchange:** Everyone anonymously writes down their expectations of teammates and leadership on index cards. Collect the cards and group them by theme. As a group, talk about each theme and reach a consensus on how to meet those expectations. Review progress monthly.

(continued)

(continued)

2. **Add to your trust account:** Have team members share specific behaviors that build or damage trust for them. Group the behaviors into Builders and Breakers and post them in a visible team space.

3. **Skill-share sessions:** For 15 minutes a week, teammates take turns teaching others something they're good at. This breaks down hierarchical barriers, creates vulnerability, and builds mutual respect.

4. **Problem-solving partners:** Pair people who need to rebuild trust and give them small, achievable projects to work on together. Include time to discuss what worked well (or didn't) in the collaboration. Rotate pairs monthly.

5. **Trust temperature check:** Every week, collect an anonymous 1–10 rating of team trust levels. Plot the results on a chart to track progress and discuss trends. Celebrate improvements and work together to solve problems that show up.

The Four Pillars of Psychological Safety

Trust, at its core, is the permission to fail. Once your team feels they have that, you can start establishing psychological safety like the team at the Four Seasons.

This is where trust really blooms. Maybe your team challenges your thinking in a meeting if someone thinks you're drifting off-track, or a team member jumps in to help you implement a solution when things go wrong. Safe teams support each other in ways that translate to better results.

So what happens when your team doesn't do this?

You probably know what this looks like—groupthink. No one ever expresses a controversial opinion or challenges the group's consensus. You may have been on a team where:

- One person's beliefs dominate the group's thinking and identity.

- The group actively avoids conflict and tries to shut down critical reactions to their decisions.

Those teams probably weren't much fun to be a part of. It's hard to feel like you're contributing when you can't challenge assumptions. Most people would agree that the best ideas come from honest discussions, healthy conflict (where you attack ideas, not the people who express them), and a tolerance for challenges.

The Yale psychologist Irving Janis has pointed out that groupthink becomes more common in highly stressful or uncertain situations.[4] Unfortunately, that's exactly when you need psychological safety. As General George Patton put it, "If everybody is thinking alike, then somebody isn't thinking."[5]

The most famous proof of the value of psychological safety is Project Aristotle, an internal study launched by Google back in 2012. Their People Operations team spent millions of dollars measuring nearly every aspect of their employees' lives—from how often people ate together to the traits of their highest-rated managers—to find out how to build "the perfect team."

At first they came up empty. After spending an entire year going through the data, there was no pattern they could find in the behavior of the 180 teams they looked at. Eventually, they found a clue in the academic literature: psychological safety. Suddenly, when the Google team looked at the data through this lens, a clear pattern emerged: This set of behaviors was the number-one predictor of team success.[6]

The results were almost shocking. People on teams with psychological safety were:

- Less likely to leave the company
- More likely to use a diverse range of ideas from their teammates
- Twice as likely to be rated effective by an executive
- More effective at bringing in revenue[7]

Creating an environment like this is not easy. As Harvard professor Amy Edmondson points out in one of her books, "Unless a leader expressly and actively makes it psychologically safe to do so, people will automatically seek to avoid failure."[8]

This makes it hard to build psychological safety. For one thing, failure pushes many people into "fight or flight." Think of how a child instinctively says, "I didn't do it!" after something breaks.

Also, while we're often told to learn from our mistakes, research shows that we pay more attention to our successes and prefer to note other people's failures rather than our own.[9]

Fortunately, research also gives us a roadmap for how to build psychological safety in teams. Let's look at four techniques you can use to create it.

How to Tell If Your Team Feels Psychological Safety

Amy Edmondson did some of the earliest research on psychological safety. One of the tools she created is a questionnaire that rates your team's level of psychological safety in four key areas:

- **Willingness to help:** How readily team members support each other
- **Inclusion and diversity:** The degree of openness to diverse perspectives

---

Happiness Works

- **Attitude to risk and failure:** Comfort with taking risks and learning from mistakes

- **Open conversation:** The ability to discuss challenges and ideas freely[10]

If you think about how well you (and your team) are showing these behaviors, you'll have a pretty good idea of your level of psychological safety and how much you trust your teammates.

Make It Okay to Fail

Failure is inevitable.

While people hate talking about failure, your team's success does not depend on what you do right—it's how you handle what goes wrong. You have to start by accepting that failure is bound to happen and it's better to focus on tackling the problem than pointing fingers.

The Glitch Report described earlier in this chapter is a great lesson because just about any team can implement their own version of it. This creates transparency and accountability that puts continuous improvement at the heart of your company culture.

By asking your team to report failures or mistakes, you can "get ahead of things" and address problems before they get too big. A reporting process tells you *why* things went wrong and gives you clues about how to fix them.

So how do you create your own Glitch Report meeting? Here's a simple four-step framework.

1. **Meet every week.** You can change the frequency depending on the kind of work you do, but the important thing is that it happens on a regular schedule.

2. **Get everyone to share one mistake.** This is crucial. It's true that everyone makes mistakes, but if some people aren't willing to admit to theirs, it's hard to build trust. This step is essential for normalizing the mistakes.

3. **Share what you learn.** A mistake that's not understood is bound to be repeated. Your goal should be to not make the same mistake twice. This means analyzing why things went wrong.

4. **Take action.** As Isadore Sharpe said, "It's not the error; it's the recovery." Analysis should come with a recommendation on how to fix the error, or an update on what action has already been taken. This tells your team that you *care* about the mistake and are doing everything possible to minimize its impact.

Taking these steps will help to create an environment where failure isn't fatal. Instead, it gives your team the courage to push through challenges and face the next one head on. By reframing failure as "successfully discovering all the ways that do not work" (to paraphrase Thomas Edison), you'll have your first pillar of psychological safety.

Model Vulnerability

Picture Detroit, 2006. Ford Motor Company was in deep trouble—bleeding money and heading toward a staggering $17 billion loss. Enter Alan Mulally, the newly recruited CEO facing what seemed like an impossible task. The company culture was toxic—executives kept problems hidden like family secrets, and departments might as well have been separate companies for all they cooperated with each other.[11]

But Mulally had a plan. He knew that without trust and transparency, Ford would keep spiraling downward. So what did he do?

He started with something deceptively simple: a mandatory Thursday morning meeting for his top 16 executives.

The setup was straightforward. Each executive had to share updates on their key projects using a traffic light system. Green meant "all good," yellow meant "we've got issues but we're on it," and red meant "we're in trouble and need help."

Now, here's where it gets interesting. At the first meeting, despite Ford practically being on fire, every single executive claimed their projects were "green." Everything's fine here, boss! Nothing to see!

The real magic happened a few weeks later. Mark Fields, who ran North American operations, did something unprecedented—he held up a red card during his report. The room froze. All eyes turned to Mulally, waiting for the explosion.

Instead, Mulally started clapping enthusiastically. "That's great visibility!" he exclaimed. In that moment, everything changed.[12]

Within weeks, the meeting room's charts looked like a Christmas tree—red and yellow everywhere. But here's the thing: Now they could finally start fixing their problems instead of pretending they didn't exist.

This wasn't just feel-good management talk—the results were incredible. While GM and Chrysler went bankrupt in 2008, Ford stayed afloat. By 2009, they weren't just surviving, they were thriving, with $2.7 billion in profit. The next year? That number jumped to $6.6 billion.[13]

The change rippled through the entire company. Instead of departments pointing fingers at each other, they started working together. Problems that used to fester for months were getting solved in less than half the time. Employee engagement doubled. People actually started looking forward to coming to work.

And it all started because one leader showed his team that it was okay—no, actually valuable—to admit when things weren't going well. Sometimes the biggest transformations start with the smallest acts of courage.

As with any new process, it only works if there is buy-in from the top.

When building psychological safety, no one is exempt from admitting failure. If you're a leader, there are a few things you can do to show this and make it easier for people to share their mistakes.

- **Praise people for admitting errors.** Praise is one of the most powerful tools a leader has, since followers naturally seek it out. Rewarding people for having the courage to share their mistakes sends a clear signal that others should follow.

- **Be the _first_ person to share a mistake.** Once other people see how you've done it, they have a model to follow. This will make them feel much more comfortable coming forward with their own errors. We all know that actions speak louder than words, so you need to show that this new practice applies to everyone.

- **Acknowledge people's fears and reframe them.** Emphasize that mistakes are a natural part of the process and what you really care about is fixing them. Use phrases like "course corrections" and "reset moments" to show that you believe the team can recover from mistakes.

It all starts from the top by showing people the right way to share failure.

Ask for Candor

Ever wonder what it feels like when some of Hollywood's most brilliant minds get together? Welcome to a typical "brain trust" meeting at Pixar Animation Studios, where brutal honesty meets creative genius, and magic happens.

Imagine walking into a meeting room at Pixar Animation Studios. The air is electric with creative tension, and around the table sit some of the most brilliant minds in animation. But this isn't your typical Hollywood pitch meeting—this is the legendary brain trust in action, and they're about to demonstrate why Pixar has become a storytelling powerhouse like no other.

Unlike other studios that buy scripts from outside writers, Pixar does something remarkable—they create every single story in-house. From *Toy Story* to *Inside Out*, each beloved tale springs from their own creative teams. But here's the fascinating part: Every single one of these masterpieces started out, in their words, kind of terrible.

"Early on, all of our movies suck," Ed Catmull, Pixar's cofounder, loves to say with surprising frankness. "Our job is to make them go . . . from suck to non-suck."[14] It's this brutally honest approach that sets Pixar apart.

The magic happens in those brain trust meetings. They go like this: A director shows their latest work-in-progress, then sits back as their peers—fellow directors, writers, and artists—spend hours delivering completely unvarnished feedback. First-time observers are often shocked by how loud and intense these sessions get. Yet listen closely and you'll hear what Catmull calls the four essential ingredients: "Frank talk, spirited debate, laughter, and love."[15]

But here's what makes this process truly special—the brain trust has absolutely no authority. Zero. Nada. Every piece of feedback, no matter how brilliant, is just a suggestion. It's like you have the world's best doctors to diagnose you—but you get to decide which prescriptions to fill.

This setup is pure genius. Because the brain trust can't force anyone to make changes, they're free to be completely honest. And because directors know they maintain full control, they're more willing to really listen. It creates this beautiful cycle of trust and candor that keeps getting stronger.

The process isn't perfect for everyone, though. Junior team members might struggle to criticize an Oscar winner's work. Introverts might find the heated discussions overwhelming. So Pixar adapted— they created additional channels for feedback, like private emails, to make sure everyone's voice could be heard.

The results? Well, they speak for themselves. Since releasing *Toy Story* (the world's first computer-animated feature) in 1995, Pixar has created 28 features that have earned a staggering $15 billion worldwide. They've collected 23 Academy Awards along the way, including 11 for Best Animated Feature. Their latest triumph, *Inside Out 2*, now holds the crown as the second-highest-grossing animated film ever made.[16]

But perhaps the most remarkable thing about Pixar's approach is how it transforms the very nature of feedback. When everyone truly believes they're working toward making something better—not just criticizing for criticism's sake—magic happens. It's not about winning arguments or proving points. It's about turning good stories into great ones, and great ones into classics.

And sometimes that process starts with being brave enough to say, "You know what? This isn't working yet. Let's figure out why."

Make Criticism Count: The Trust-Feedback Loop

The most powerful feedback often stings the most, but only if we're willing to hear it. While organizations spend countless hours designing feedback frameworks and processes, they often miss a fundamental truth: Trust determines whether feedback lands softly or detonates.

When we trust someone, their criticism becomes valuable intelligence about our blind spots from someone invested in our success. Trust is the backbone of feedback. Without trust, even the most carefully worded suggestion feels like an attack, and our brains treat it like a threat rather than an opportunity to grow. It's why the same piece of feedback (such as "your communication style is causing problems") can feel either like a personal assault or a crucial insight, depending entirely on who delivers it and the trust you share.

Trust transforms feedback from a threat into intelligence. When feedback comes from someone you trust, you're getting valuable data from a person who wants you to succeed. They've likely thought carefully about what to say and how to say it. They're taking a risk by being honest with you. That's different from random criticism from someone who doesn't understand your context or care about your growth.

But here's the tricky part: Sometimes the most valuable feedback comes from people you don't particularly like or trust. Maybe they see blind spots that your allies miss. The key is to evaluate both the message and the messenger. What's their expertise? What are their motives? Do they have relevant context? Sometimes a critic can be right for the wrong reasons.

Instead of using complex feedback models, focus on three things:

1. **Pause before reacting.** Your brain will scream "Threat!" Take a breath. Thank them. Ask questions. Sleep on major feedback if you can.

2. **Mine for specifics.** Vague feedback is useless feedback. "Your presentations could be better" tells you nothing. Push for examples: "Which presentation? What specifically didn't work?"

3. **Close the loop.** Tell them what you'll do differently and actually do it. Nothing builds trust like showing that feedback leads to positive change.

Remember: The goal isn't to get comfortable with criticism; it's to get better at your job. When you trust the feedback process, you can focus less on defending yourself and more on growing. That's when feedback becomes a superpower rather than a source of stress.

The Journey to Trust

The road to trust is a lot like the road to happiness: Both are paved with small, consistent actions. If you're like me, you probably don't trust big statements or grand gestures—it never feels like they amount to much. But doing the right thing over and over again is a magic formula for making trust stronger.

Those right things are demonstrating your capability and character, over and over again. Every time you put the work in to deliver a flawless presentation, people's trust in you increases. When you stay late to help your teammate get their crucial project over the line before the deadline, that support tells your team that you won't let them fail.

Those small actions compound over time. If you can focus on building a little bit of trust with your colleagues every day, you'll start earning a "happiness dividend"—you'll have more friends at work, more support, and more recognition. You'll feel free to take more risks. Most importantly, your team will believe in you and you'll believe in them. As we saw with the Four Seasons and Pixar, it's supporting each other that lets your team accomplish great things.

The Happiness, Works Method: Trust and Psychological Safety

- **Schedule your "Glitch Report" meeting.** Encourage your team to embrace psychological safety by experimenting with different ways to share mistakes. Using the Glitch Report as a model, build transparency and accountability in your team by making it easy for every person to share at least one mistake or failure. Soon your whole team will be building trust by sharing insights and getting ahead of problems before they get too large.

- **Find opportunities to build trust.** Teams trust each other more when they practice trust-building habits together. Creating opportunities for people to collaborate, and recognizing team members who build trust, get everyone pulling in the same direction.

- **Assess trust on your team and diagnose any problems.** You have to look for the signs of eroding trust, whether that be through feedback or recognizing distrustful behaviors. Quick interventions will reinforce trust by showing that mistakes get corrected.

- **Try a "brain trust" meeting.** Candor requires permission and a bit of thick skin. Explain the brain trust concept to your team and assemble a group to try it on one of your team's projects (maybe yours!). It's much easier to see the benefits for a project if you put radical trust into practice.

- **Practice receiving constructive criticism.** It's easy to read what you should do when someone critiques your work, but you won't know if you've really learned it until you try. Seek out some constructive criticism and see how well you handle it. It won't necessarily be easy, but it will certainly help you grow.

Chapter 6

The Sweet Spot of Progress

I slide into my chair at the gleaming conference table in PepsiCo's Mumbai office, where the afternoon sun streams through floor-to-ceiling windows. The air is thick with anticipation and the mingling aromas of dozens of open chip bags scattered around the room. My fingers brush against a bag of Magic Masala Lay's as I reach for my notebook and I catch a whiff of cardamom and cumin.

Around me, the product development team shifts uncomfortably in their seats. Ramesh, the senior marketing director, drums his fingers on the table next to a pile of market research reports. Kelly from R&D keeps rearranging the samples of experimental flavors—Chai Spice, Hot & Sweet Chili, Spanish Tomato Tango—like pieces on a chess board she can't quite figure out.

The pressure in the room is palpable. We're not just creating another snack; we're trying to innovate for Lay's—a market leader that seems to have already conquered every conceivable flavor combination. The weight of this responsibility sits heavy on our shoulders, like the humid Mumbai air.

I watch as Maya, the junior product manager, picks up a Chile Limon chip, studies it, then puts it back with a sigh. We've been at this for hours. Days. The whiteboard is covered with crossed-out ideas, and the energy that buzzed through the room this morning has fizzled into frustrated silence. We're drowning in possibilities, paralyzed by potential, each of us secretly wondering if we're the one holding the team back.

Does this churning stomach, racing mind, and overwhelming pressure feel familiar? Have you ever sat in a room where creativity was supposed to flow freely, but instead you felt trapped by expectations?

Fortunately for us (and chip lovers everywhere), we stumbled upon a *game-changer*.

I'm sure you're familiar with to-do lists. We had those but, in a moment of inspiration, we flipped this concept on its head.

Here's what we did: We took all of the things we needed to do and wrote them on Post-it Notes. Then we plastered these all over the wall behind us until we had hundreds of pastel-colored squares. But this wasn't our to-do list. We called it our "Done List."

You might be thinking, "How are a bunch of unfinished tasks a Done List?" Simple: Every time we completed a task, no matter how small, we'd move that Post-it from the To-Do side to the Done side. As strange as it sounds, there's something incredibly satisfying about physically moving that little square of paper across the room.

It might sound straightforward, but it made a difference. Suddenly, we could see our progress right there on the wall. It was like a constantly growing monument to our hard work. That feeling of progress, seeing our Done side fill up, gave us momentum. It kept our spirits high and our energy up, even when we were knee-deep in chip flavors and market research.

Our Done List became more than just a list of completed tasks. It was like a record of our journey, a visual story of our success. Every Post-it on that Done side represented a small victory, a step forward. And all those small victories? They added up to something big.

This simple act changed our whole perspective. Instead of feeling overwhelmed by what we still had to do, we felt motivated by what we'd already accomplished. It was like we had proof, right there on the wall, that we were making progress, that we were capable of getting things done.

The progress we made was about more than new product ideas. Suddenly we were working together. We started building on each other's ideas. The energy in the room was electric. We went from dreading our brainstorming sessions to looking forward to them. We even started having fun.

And here's the real magic: This progress, this momentum, fed on itself. The more progress we made, the more confident we felt. The more confident we felt, the more risks we were willing to take. And the more risks we took, the more innovative our ideas became.

By the end of the project, we hadn't just come up with a list of new snack ideas. We'd transformed how we worked as a team.

Looking back, I realize that what we achieved with Pepsi in India wasn't just about new snack flavors. It was about unlocking the potential that was there all along. It was about creating an environment where progress was inevitable and, most importantly, visible.

The Done List is something you can apply anywhere, whether you're in a classroom, a boardroom, or anywhere in between. When you focus on progress, when you make it visible and celebrate it, that's when you start to see real momentum. That's when you start to see what your team is really capable of.

The Done List is also an example of one of the fundamental truths of workplace happiness. It's called the "progress principle."

The Progress Principle

Harvard professor Teresa Amabile literally wrote the book on the progress principle. For the book, she gave people "work diaries" where they made more than 12,000 entries. When she reviewed these entries, she realized that they contained a fundamental truth about human motivation. The notes were intimate windows into the daily lives of 250 professionals across seven companies, each page filled with raw emotions, honest reflections, and unfiltered thoughts about their work and colleagues.[1]

As Amabile sifted through these personal accounts, one question kept drawing her attention: "Describe one event that occurred today that stands out in your mind." The answer hit her like a lightning bolt—it wasn't money, recognition, or even praise that made people's days great.

It was progress. A staggering 76 percent of people's best days hinged on that simple feeling of moving forward.[2]

Think about your own workday. Remember that last time you crossed something off your list and felt that tiny surge of satisfaction? That's not just satisfaction—it's your brain's reward system at work. Like a surfer catching a wave, each small win creates momentum. Progress sparks happiness, happiness fuels creativity, and creativity drives even more progress. It's a virtuous cycle that can transform your entire work experience.

But there's a dark side: When that progress stalls, it's like being trapped in quicksand. We've all felt that hamster-wheel sensation, where you're expending energy but going nowhere. Your brain, wired for growth and forward motion, starts to rebel. Boredom creeps in. Focus slips away. Your work starts to feel like a weight.

The real magic happens when people can see their impact. Progress is not just about checking boxes; it's about witnessing how your daily efforts ripple out into the world. Amabile found that the highest satisfaction comes from this potent combination of earned achievement and meaningful contribution. Each visible step forward releases a hit of dopamine, but more importantly, it feeds our deep-seated need for purpose.

Think of progress like a snowball rolling downhill. Each small win adds to its size and momentum. But unlike a snowball, progress can be fragile. Sometimes it's blocked by others—that colleague who hasn't responded to your urgent email, or the resource request that's been sitting in approval limbo. Sometimes we're our own worst enemies, falling into the procrastination trap when tasks don't feel meaningful enough.

The key? Keep moving forward, even if it's just baby steps. As Isaac Newton observed about objects in motion, progress tends to create more progress. The question is: How do we start that motion and keep it going?

We'll spend the rest of the chapter diving into specific tactics you can use to build progress, but I like to use the metaphor of the campfire. You need to create the right conditions to keep the fire burning.

- **Make progress visible.** Instead of abstract goals like "improve team communication," track specific actions. (For example, "I had three meaningful one-on-ones this week.") Each small win fuels the next.

- **Focus on enjoyment.** Teams that harness what energizes them are more productive. Progress should make things feel easier and easier as you build up momentum.

- **Celebrate progress, not just outcomes.** We'll talk more about what psychologists call "progress rituals"—regular moments to acknowledge movement forward. The Done List becomes more powerful when it includes not just what you did, but what you enjoyed about doing it.

Let's look at some proven ways you can keep the fire of progress burning.

Building Momentum Toward More Progress

For progress to happen, we need to set goals that matter to us and understand how we're moving toward those goals. When we don't, that feeling of going through the motions seeps in—we're direction-less, demotivated, and hurtling toward depression.

Fortunately, there's a better way. Once you start building momentum, progress feels easy and natural. You just have to know how to build it.

The Power of Purpose: Stop Searching, Start Serving

Ever had that moment when someone asks you about your life's purpose and your mind goes completely blank? Yeah, I've been there. It's like being asked to solve world peace over cold pizza at 3 a.m.—overwhelming and slightly anxiety-inducing.

But what if we're asking the wrong question entirely? Instead of getting lost in the philosophical maze of "finding your purpose," ask yourself: Who needs you? More specifically, what are you doing for others that they simply couldn't do without you?

Amy is a software developer I know. She used to struggle with the whole "purpose" thing until she realized something powerful: Her code wasn't just lines on a screen, it was helping small business owners sleep better at night, knowing their financial data was secure and organized. Suddenly, her work wasn't just a job anymore—it became a mission.

This brings us to the million-dollar follow-up: What kind of impact are you actually having on these people? You might be showing up, but without that connection to real impact, something vital is missing.

Think about it: When was the last time you felt truly energized at work? Chances are it wasn't when you were mindlessly checking boxes off a to-do list. According to recent research, people who see their work benefiting others have measurably higher job satisfaction and performance.[3] Even more mind-blowing? Those who use their strengths daily to serve others are six times more likely to be engaged. Six times![4]

Let me share a quick story: One of my clients, Marcus, worked in customer service for years feeling "meh" about his job. Then he started keeping a folder of thank-you messages from customers he'd helped out of tough situations. Each message was a reminder that he wasn't just answering phones—he was being someone's hero on what might have been their worst day. His entire outlook transformed.

Ready to supercharge your own sense of purpose? Try these action steps:

- **Become an impact detective.** Track your work like a detective following leads. Who's using what you create? What falls apart if you don't show up? One marketing manager I know discovered her market research didn't just inform decisions—it helped preserve jobs by steering the company away from costly mistakes. She just hadn't connected those dots before.

- **Turn your wins into stories.** Got positive feedback? Don't just file it away—share it! When your colleague handles a crisis brilliantly, tell that story. These aren't just feel-good moments; they're proof that your work matters. Impact stories create a positive feedback loop that energizes entire teams.

- **Give yourself objectives, not tasks.** Instead of writing "complete quarterly report," write "equip leadership team to make confident decisions about our next market expansion." See how that hits differently? You're not just completing tasks; you're creating real-world impact.

Remember, purpose isn't some mystical destination—it's happening right now, in the way you show up and serve others. What will you do today that someone else couldn't do without you?

The Sweet Spot of Progress

The Unappreciated Motivation Tool

Teresa Amabile and her team gave a survey to 669 leaders from dozens of companies around the world. These leaders came from a range of management levels and were asked to rank five potential employee motivators:

1. Support for making progress in work
2. Recognition for good work
3. Incentives
4. Interpersonal support
5. Clear goals

- **The critical finding:** Only 5 percent of leaders ranked "support for progress" as the top motivator. Instead, most leaders believed that recognition (praise) was the most important motivator for employees.[5]

- **The irony:** The research found that making meaningful progress in one's work is the most powerful motivator for employees. So there's a stark mismatch between what actually motivates employees (progress) and what leaders think motivates employees (recognition).

- **The implications:** This misunderstanding likely leads to suboptimal management approaches. Leaders might focus too heavily on giving praise while underinvesting in removing obstacles and supporting actual progress in work. This could explain why many employees remain unmotivated despite receiving recognition. They're not getting what they truly need most—support for making meaningful progress in their work.

Making Quick Decisions: Maximizers versus Satisficers

The way we approach decision-making has a profound impact on our ability to make progress, yet this connection is often overlooked. Many people get trapped in decision-making patterns that actually hinder their forward momentum, turning what should be steppingstones into roadblocks. This is particularly evident in the distinction between maximizers and satisficers—two fundamentally different approaches to making choices that can either accelerate or impede progress.

Are You a Maximizer or a Satisficer?

Maximizers are individuals who strive to make the "perfect" choice, exhaustively searching for and evaluating all possible options before deciding. While this might sound thorough, it often leads to:

- Decision paralysis from information overload
- Increased stress and anxiety
- Delayed action and reduced progress
- Greater likelihood of regret, even after making good choices
- Constant second-guessing of decisions made

Satisficers, on the other hand, make decisions based on finding options that meet their core criteria—what's "good enough" rather than "perfect." This approach typically results in:

- Faster decision-making
- Reduced cognitive load
- Greater satisfaction with choices
- More energy focused on implementation rather than selection
- Better progress due to maintaining forward momentum[6]

Picture yourself standing in a grocery store, staring at 47 different types of breakfast cereal. Twenty minutes later, you're still there, reading nutrition labels and comparing prices per ounce, while your ice cream melts in the cart. Sound familiar? You might be a maximizer—someone who's determined to make the absolutely perfect choice, even if it means turning a simple decision into an epic quest.

Meanwhile, your friend breezes in, grabs the first reasonably healthy cereal that's on sale, and is home enjoying breakfast before you've even made it to the checkout line. She's a satisficer—she knows what she needs and isn't tortured by the possibility that another option might have been marginally better.

This isn't just about breakfast choices. The way we make decisions shapes everything about our progress in life. Maximizers are like amateur photographers who spend so much time adjusting their camera settings that they miss the perfect sunset. They're paralyzed by options, haunted by "what-ifs," and often end up more stressed and less satisfied, even when they make objectively good choices.

Satisficers, by contrast, are like surfers who catch the first good wave instead of waiting for the perfect one that may never come. They're not settling for mediocrity—they're pragmatic about what "good enough" looks like, and they use their energy to move forward rather than second-guessing themselves.

Think about the last major decision you made. Did you find yourself going down endless research rabbit holes, asking everyone you know for advice, and still feeling uncertain? Or did you identify your key criteria, find a solid option that met them, and move forward with confidence? Your answer might tell you a lot about why some decisions energize you while others drain your will to live.

So Which Method Works Better?

That really depends on what you want. In general, maximizers achieve better outcomes, but satisficers are happier with their choices.[7]

Well, that's weird.

You would think that achieving the best outcome—picking the "right" job, finding the perfect watch, or ordering the perfect dish at a new restaurant—would make you happier. But how quickly you make the decision has a big impact on how happy you are with the result.

Maximizers agonize over their choices. They have more stress and more anxiety, and they get stuck in decision paralysis. Once they make their choice, they can't stop evaluating whether it was the "right" one.

Satisficers make decisions quickly and have less anxiety. They're more content with their choices because they accept that perfect usually isn't possible. This more laid-back attitude leads to more progress and ultimately more happiness.

The difference really stands out when we're faced with a lot of options. In his book *The Paradox of Choice*, Barry Schwarz shows that our happiness goes down when our number of choices goes up. The research that proves this is known as the "jam study." It found that shoppers who had to choose among 24 different varieties of jam were less satisfied with their choice than people who were given six options.[8]

Maximizing might lead to marginally better decisions, but the cost in time, energy, and happiness often isn't worth it. Satisficers want what they have, while maximizers are always chasing what they want.

Steppingstones to Happiness

So what does this have to do with progress and how happy you are at work?

Think about making progress like using steppingstones to cross a river. Maximizers spend so much time analyzing each stone's position that they often stay stuck on one bank. Satisficers keep moving forward by finding stones that are "good enough."

This has *huge* implications for how to be happy at work. Teams who embrace a "good enough" approach complete more projects. By satisficing, they have less decision fatigue, and by avoiding perfectionism they can do quicker iterations that lead to faster learning and improvement. This gets the flywheel of progress spinning, which then becomes a source of momentum and satisfaction.

So instead of trying to perfect every email, presentation, and decision, learn to think in "thresholds":

- What's the minimum viable version of what I'm working on?
- When does "good enough" achieve my goal or move things forward?
- Will putting in an extra effort create a big enough return?

This doesn't mean that you should ship your first draft to customers or clients (it wouldn't be good enough to meet your goal), but it does mean that you should think about the trade-offs between your effort and your results. Sometimes done is better than perfect.

Teams who embrace satisficing often get better results because they:

- Maintain momentum
- Get feedback earlier and learn from it
- Build confidence as they pile up "wins"
- Avoid burnout from endless optimization

Progress feeds on progress. Each "good enough" step propels you forward to the next one.

Designing Your Day: From Ordinary to Extraordinary

Ever catch yourself zoning out at work, mechanically clicking through emails while your dreams gather digital dust in some forgotten folder? You're not alone. Research shows we're all stuck on autopilot for at least half our day—and that's a recipe for staying stuck.[9]

When you're running on autopilot, asking, "How can we solve this problem?" is like asking a GPS to find a creative shortcut—you'll just get the same old route you've always taken. Innovation? Creativity? They're taking a nap while you're on cruise control.

Breaking free from autopilot doesn't require a grand gesture. Think of it like hitting your body's reset button: Take that walk around the block (yes, even in the rain), actually leave your desk for lunch (your sandwich will taste better, I promise), or have that random coffee chat with the colleague whose energy always lifts you up. The goal? To snap out of your routine at least three times a day. Your creativity will thank you.

Things get really interesting when we start adding "progress loops," your secret weapon for turning good days into great ones. They work like this: You make meaningful progress, acknowledge it (this part is crucial!), feel that little burst of accomplishment, and BAM—suddenly you're firing on all cylinders, full of momentum and ready to tackle even bigger challenges.

I saw this transformation with Jamie, a developer who started keeping a "victory wall" in her home office. Every time she solved a tricky bug or helped a teammate, she'd add it to her wall. Within weeks, her confidence soared and her productivity followed. Why? Because she could literally see her impact growing day by day.

Ready to design your own breakthrough day? Here's your action plan:

- **Choose your daily quest.** Start each morning by picking one meaningful goal that would make the day count. It doesn't have to be massive—it could simply be helping a new team member or finally tackling that project that's been nagging at you. The key is that it matters to you.

- **Align your actions with your truth.** Think of your values as your internal compass. If creativity matters to you, how can you inject more innovation into your daily tasks? If connection is your thing, how can you make your meetings more engaging? When your actions match your values, even mundane tasks become meaningful.

- **Create ripples of impact.** Feeling stuck on your big goals? Zoom in on the small ways you can make someone's day better. Maybe it's taking time to mentor a junior colleague, sharing your expertise in a team meeting, or simply sending that encouraging message to someone who's struggling. These micro-impacts add up to major momentum.

The beauty of designing your day this way is that it turns the ordinary into the extraordinary. You're not just checking boxes anymore—you're creating impact, building momentum, and actually enjoying the journey.

So, what's your first step off autopilot going to be?

The Beauty of Bite-Sized Milestones

Everyone wants a big win.

Don't get me wrong—big wins are great. They're huge motivators and you chase them because they're meaningful. But they also pose a few problems. They don't happen often. They're hard to achieve and usually take a lot of time. And they often depend on things that are out of your control.

That doesn't mean we shouldn't aim for big wins, but there's a better way to get there.

As we saw with the Done List earlier in this chapter, small achievements are dominoes that lead to bigger glory. By breaking our big goals into bite-sized chunks, we gain some important things. More control. A higher success rate. Daily dopamine. Momentum.

In short, setting bite-sized, daily goals give us positive feelings and better results. But the reasons that small goals are important run much deeper:

- **Small successes give you a sense of control.** If you start each day by accomplishing your most important goal for that day, it helps you feel autonomy and makes you feel good about yourself. If you think back to the hierarchy of happiness from Chapter 2, autonomy and accomplishment are both important parts of personal growth, the second-highest block on the pyramid. Feeling in control has been proven to boost your motivation and improve results.[10]

- **Every win makes you believe in yourself.** The power of winning is that it increases something psychologists call "self-efficacy"—your belief that you can successfully complete a task. You are more likely to attempt a task if you think you'll accomplish it. The more you think you'll succeed, the more effort, persistence, and resilience you'll put in when faced with obstacles.[11] For managers, this virtuous cycle is like a cheat code—set up your team to succeed and focus on improving each team member's self-belief. The wins will naturally follow.

- **"Micro-habits" lead to lasting change.** Sabina Nawaz coaches CEOs on how to achieve big things. One of the most common mistakes she sees is that people try to go too big, too fast. Everyone wants to make a dramatic change overnight, but when the enthusiasm dies out a couple of weeks later, the change is too hard or intimidating and people quit. Instead, she tells her clients to practice "micro-habits," which are small components of a larger habit. When she set a goal to run a 10K, her first habit was laying out her gym clothes at night and putting them on right away in the morning. When she got to the gym, she spent just 10 minutes walking on the treadmill. The treadmill time gradually increased, as did the pace, and she followed those steps over several months until she could run 10K. The key was to gradually build confidence. She never increased the goal by more than 10 percent every couple of weeks.[12]

- **Progress leads to fulfillment.** The more people feel a sense of progress, the more likely they are to be creatively productive in the long run.[13] In other words, it's not just about making good things happen more often—if you make progress a habit, the quality of your accomplishments will also rise. This is how growth leads to fulfillment. As you gain confidence, enthusiasm, and the ability to handle larger challenges, you become more likely to reach the top rung of the happiness hierarchy—meaning and fulfillment.

Fulfillment can feel a long way away when you start with small goals. But hitting these bite-sized milestones will get you climbing the ladder of achievement. Eventually, your momentum will propel you to the top.

Take action. Start small. The action is more important than the goal. Just get started.

Choose Your Goals Wisely

Nothing will stall progress like picking goals that can't be achieved. You shouldn't "sandbag" and only go after easy problems, but you have to avoid goals that don't deliver that pinch of progress. Here are three negative goals that can kill your momentum.

1. **Goals that aren't very likely:** Nothing will kill momentum faster than a goal that's doomed to fail. These failures can have a lasting impact: The negative effects of setbacks are three times stronger than the positive impacts of progress.[14]

2. **Goals with a lot of emotional power:** The higher the emotion, the higher the risk. It's not just that missing an emotion-packed goal can be devastating; even the high of achieving that goal is often followed by "arrival fallacy." That's the inevitable letdown you feel when the elation of achieving the big goal wears off.[15]

3. **Goals that we don't control:** When your goals depend on factors that are out of your hands—like how well your competitors perform in a competition—you're measuring yourself against a moving target. Known in the literature as "normative comparison," these kinds of goals increase your sense of unease (because you don't have control) and usually hurt your performance.[16]

The right goals focus on processes, not outcomes. Going one step at a time (rather than fretting about a far-off result) reduces your anxiety.[17]

Handling Setbacks: Don't Get Derailed

I just mentioned how setbacks pack a big punch, which can quickly undermine the benefits of progress. And there will be setbacks—it's impossible for everything to go right for long. If you're serious about achieving your goals, you need a strategy for minimizing the impact of these setbacks.

The good news is that you have control over how negativity affects you. As we saw in Chapter 4, learning resilience will keep you on track and stop you from losing too much momentum when things don't go as planned.

One of my favorite strategies for preventing setbacks comes from Dale Carnegie, whose books (like the timeless classic *How to Win Friends and Influence People*) date back to the 1930s. Carnegie says we must learn to live in day-tight compartments. What does that mean? It means staying aware of future goals but living in the present.

Living in day-tight compartments is an analogy from the world of ocean liners, where the captain, if there is a leak, will just press a button and big heavy iron doors will close off sections of the ship— creating watertight compartments. As long as those doors are closed, even a leaking ship will be very hard to sink.

You get the idea: If there is a problem (or a leak) in your mind, bring down the metal doors and close off the mental compartments that are causing it—all the what-if's and worries that can throw us off course (or even sink us). This will give you the peace of mind to focus on today and move forward. By living in day-tight compartments, you're creating a mental "off switch" for your worries and an "on switch" for your focus. There is nothing particularly new or advanced about this, but it is incredibly effective.

I learned this the hard way. When I was in college, I was part of the theater department. The University of Pennsylvania was not a school necessarily known for its theater department, but they wanted to change that and build a new theater. It was a big deal.

At one performance, a bunch of important alumni were invited to be in the audience. I was backstage and our stage manager, armed with her clipboard, told me to go change for my next scene.

You know when you think to yourself, "Really? Now? That doesn't feel right." But she had the clipboard, so clearly she was the expert. I did what I always do (I'm a rule follower) and went backstage to start changing into my next costume.

A few minutes later, the clipboard reappears. She's in a bit of panic. Really more than a bit of a panic. She tells me that I am due on stage *right now*. I am literally half-dressed and the zipper on my dress is not moving.

I thought to myself: I have two choices. I could leave—there's a back door right over there. Or I could go back on stage and close the metal doors of my mind—containing all of my anxieties and worries to one section of my brain.

I went on stage to my poor scene partner (who looked like she wanted to kill me) and I held my dress closed with one hand. I brought down the metal doors on my anxiety and put it in a compartment, keeping my embarrassment confined to a distant corner of my mind. I finished my monologue with one hand on the back of my dress (praying for no wardrobe malfunctions). But I didn't let that ship sink.

How to Be an Uninspiring Leader

Even a leader with the best intentions can undermine team morale. How many of these five common mistakes are killing your team's energy, productivity, and progress?

1. **Changing your mind:** It's impossible to follow an erratic leader. Constant flip-flopping leads to a lot of effort and little progress. As a leader, take time to think through your decisions, rather than giving in to the instinct to "do something" and act fast. You want to "measure twice, cut once," especially on important issues.

2. **Never changing your mind:** The chance that you're always right is zero. If you've invested in hiring people more talented

(continued)

(continued)

than you (which should be your goal), listen to them when they tell you to change course. Make sure your team has feedback rituals to make it easy for them to weigh in, and delegate decisions to the people closest to the issue.

3. **Having a lack of direction:** Elite performers don't want a job—they want a mission. It's hard to sign up for a journey to nowhere. As a leader, it's your job to ruthlessly eliminate work that isn't mission-aligned and to build coherent stories about your mission that become mythology.

4. **Playing unwinnable games:** We all want to win. But we can't if we don't know the rules or those rules are not consistent. (Don't be the kid who changes the rules when they lose.) Create a scoreboard for your team that is public and visible, so everyone knows where they stand. Everyone, regardless of role, should be targeting a number they can beat.

5. **Tolerating mediocrity:** A-players want to work with A-players to grow. B-players want to work with C-players to look good. Your job is to build a culture around high standards and mutual accountability that makes everyone want to be an A-player.

The Happiness, Works Method: Progress

- **Connect with your purpose.** Use who benefits from your work to fuel your progress. Forging closer ties with the customers (or coworkers) you serve will energize you by putting a spotlight on the value you're providing and making your work feel more meaningful.

- **Be a satisficer.** Satisficers look for the "good enough" option. This lets them make quicker iterations, complete more projects, and avoid burnout. Learn to think about problems as "thresholds" and keep yourself and your team moving forward.

- **Build your progress loops.** Look for ways to incorporate progress into your daily routine. This could be anything from your own version of the Done List to taking on your biggest goal for the day before anything else.

- **Think small.** While everyone wants to accomplish their "big hairy audacious goals," creating a series of small wins is what will give you momentum. Setting bite-sized goals will make winning a habit.

- **Don't get derailed.** Setbacks are three times more powerful than progress. Stay on course by learning how to make your mind a "day-tight container" and keep yourself on track when things get hard.

Chapter 7

Hope and a Plan
The Power of Optimism

Fifty-six hours into what was supposed to be a routine mission, the screens of the NASA control room were filled with disaster warnings. Apollo 13 was in serious trouble—and three astronauts' lives hung in the balance. The lunar landing mission had suffered a catastrophic failure, oxygen was venting into space, and power was failing.

"Okay, Houston, we've had a problem here," came the calm voice of astronaut Jack Swigert over the radio.[1]

Flight Director Gene Kranz gathered his team and delivered the message that would define NASA's culture for generations: "We've never lost an American in space; we're sure as hell not going to lose one on my watch! Failure is not an option."[2]

What followed was a masterclass in optimistic problem-solving. The team faced seemingly impossible challenges: dwindling oxygen, plummeting temperatures, rising carbon dioxide, and the need to navigate a damaged spacecraft precisely back to Earth using minimal power.

Against all odds, Apollo 13 splashed down safely in the Pacific Ocean on April 17, 1970. What NASA called a "successful failure" demonstrated how the combination of technical excellence and resolute optimism could transform potential tragedy into triumph.

This is optimism at work: maintaining conviction that solutions exist even when they aren't yet visible. And the good news? Optimism isn't just an innate trait—it's a skill that can be developed through deliberate practice, strengthened like any other capability through consistent training and application.

This same practical optimism shaped another iconic American success story, though in a completely different arena.

In the early 1970s, George Lucas pitched a space fantasy film to skeptical studio executives. Despite his previous success with *American Graffiti*, sci-fi wasn't popular, and his vision for *Star Wars* seemed far-fetched. When 20th Century Fox finally agreed to a modest deal ($15,000 for development, $50,000 for the script, and $100,000 to direct), they agreed to throw in something they considered worthless: the merchandising and sequel rights.[3]

That strategic decision—born of practical optimism rather than blind faith—transformed Lucas into a billionaire and revolutionized the film industry's approach to licensing. The success of *Star Wars* merchandise generated billions, far exceeding the film's box office revenue.

When I share this story, someone inevitably mutters, "Yeah, but that's George Lucas." This misses the point entirely. Before becoming an icon, he was simply a filmmaker with an unusual vision who was facing constant rejection. What distinguished him wasn't just talent—it was clear-eyed, practical optimism about potential opportunities others couldn't see.

Whether in a life-or-death crisis at NASA or in the strategic vision of a filmmaker, optimism isn't about denying reality—it's about engaging with it more effectively. It's about maintaining the conviction that solutions exist, even when you can't see them yet.

Beyond the Motivational Poster

Many of my clients look at me with a side-eye when I suggest optimism as a key to workplace success. I can see their eyes glaze over, imagining motivational posters of soaring eagles and morning affirmations in the mirror. "I'm a realist," they declare, as if optimism and realism were somehow at war with each other. One CEO recently told me, "In my industry, we can't afford to be optimistic." Six months later, after implementing my practical optimism strategies, his company had its best quarter in five years.

I've seen it a thousand times. The moment I mention "optimism" in a corporate setting, eyebrows shoot up and arms cross defensively. You can practically hear the internal eye rolls. One hard-nosed executive actually laughed out loud.

Here's what the skeptics miss: Practical optimism isn't about denying reality, it's about engaging with it more effectively. Think of it as your problem-solving superpower. When faced with a challenge, pessimists see walls, while practical optimists see puzzles to be solved. Both see the same reality, but their approach to it differs fundamentally.

The science backs this up. Optimists aren't just happier—they're more successful. They handle problems head-on, maintain better health, earn more, and build stronger relationships.[4] They even live longer, with multiple long-term studies showing that optimistic people have a 15 percent longer lifespan and a 50 percent greater chance of reaching age 85 compared to their pessimistic counterparts.[5]

Sustained success in any field requires persisting through failure, adapting to challenges, and maintaining enthusiasm in the face of setbacks. That's not blind positivity; it's practical optimism at work.

For all these reasons, it's almost impossible to succeed without optimism. And here's the truly inspiring part: This superpower is available to every single one of us. When you embrace practical optimism, you're not just changing your mindset—you're unlocking your potential to transform challenges into opportunities, setbacks into comebacks, and ordinary careers into extraordinary ones.

The Power of Optimism at Work

"But how can I be optimistic when everything's falling apart?"

That's what I hear from overwhelmed people dealing with crushing workloads, overwhelming stress, and constant pressure. They're exhausted, uncertain, and skeptical when I suggest optimism as the solution.

Here's the thing: Optimism is a strategic mindset that transforms how you tackle challenges. Practical optimism equips you with a toolkit for dismantling obstacles, recognizing hidden patterns, and constructing innovative solutions. It's the difference between hoping things will work out and engineering conditions where success becomes virtually inevitable.

In one study, researchers followed 219 students in an online accounting course. The optimistic students didn't just ace their exams—they approached the entire course differently. They set achievable goals, planned proactively, and doubled down when things got tough. Their optimism wasn't just an attitude—it was a strategy.[6]

Now, if you're thinking, "That's great, but I was born a pessimist," I have liberating news: Your brain isn't locked into permanent pessimism. In my work with former "professional pessimists," I've seen remarkable transformations within just 60 days of consistent practice. One financial analyst who described himself as "allergic to optimism" discovered that by using my very specific techniques, he could systematically convert catastrophic thinking into strategic problem-solving. Six months later, his colleagues voted him "most constructive team member" without knowing about his optimism training.

One of the cognitive reframing techniques I recommend is the "temporary, specific, nonpersonal" method, which helps to transform pessimistic thinking patterns. It involves breaking down negative thoughts into three components:

1. **Temporary:** Recognize that the challenging situation or feeling is not permanent. Instead of seeing problems as endless, frame them as having a beginning and an end.

2. **Specific:** Focus on the particular circumstances rather than generalizing. Instead of "everything is falling apart," identify exactly what isn't working in this specific situation.

3. **Nonpersonal:** Separate the problem from your identity. Rather than "I'm a failure," recognize that the situation doesn't define you as a person.

For example, instead of thinking, "I always mess up important presentations because I'm just not good enough" (permanent, general, and personal), you might reframe it as "This presentation didn't go as planned because I didn't allocate enough preparation time this week, but I can approach the next one differently" (temporary, specific, and nonpersonal).

This method helps break the cycle of pessimistic thinking by creating space for constructive problem-solving and realistic optimism.

Techniques like these create a powerful cycle: Optimism leads to positive interactions, which increases engagement, boosts job satisfaction, and reinforces your optimistic outlook. It's not just positive thinking—it's a practical tool for transforming your work life.

Practical Optimism in Action: From Classrooms to Emergency Rooms

When Linda took over as principal at an elementary school, the school was among the lowest performing in the district. Teacher turnover exceeded 40 percent annually, test scores had declined for five straight years, and parent involvement was almost nonexistent.

"The first thing most people told me was everything we couldn't do," Linda recalls. "We had no budget, challenging demographics, and demoralized staff."

Linda and I spent hours talking about how practical optimism could help her with these seemingly insurmountable challenges. Rather than accepting these limitations, Linda began by creating a "bright spots" map—identifying pockets of excellence already existing within the struggling school. She discovered a fourth-grade teacher whose students consistently outperformed expectations, a custodian who had created an unofficial mentoring program, and a parent volunteer who spoke five languages.

"Instead of focusing on what was broken, we amplified what was working," she told me. "We created systems to spread these successful practices throughout the school."

Linda implemented peer-to-peer learning where teachers observed their colleagues' successful techniques. She formalized the custodian's mentoring program, providing him with training and making student mentorship part of his official responsibilities. The multilingual parent became their parent engagement coordinator, dramatically improving communication with families.

Within three years, teacher retention improved dramatically, test scores rose consistently, and parent involvement tripled. When I asked her how she did it, she told me, "Practical optimism in education isn't about ignoring problems—it's about believing that solutions already exist within your community if you look carefully enough."

This same approach transformed healthcare delivery in a hospital emergency department.

"Our wait times were approaching six hours, and both patients and providers were suffering," a doctor I was working with told me.

"The easy response would have been to blame the system and maintain the status quo."

Instead, the doctor applied practical optimism to healthcare delivery. Rather than requesting additional resources (which weren't available), he implemented a "split-flow" model that categorized patients by acuity and created separate treatment pathways. He empowered nurses to initiate certain protocols before physician assessment and reorganized physical spaces to improve efficiency.

"The most powerful change came from our daily problem-solving sessions," he explained to me. "We gathered for just 15 minutes each morning to identify one small improvement we could implement immediately."

These incremental changes—a revised triage form, repositioned supply cabinets, standardized discharge instructions—accumulated into remarkable results. Within six months, average wait times decreased significantly, provider satisfaction scores improved, and patient complaints dropped.

Both Linda and the doctor demonstrate a crucial truth about practical optimism: It's not about denying challenges but rather approaching them with the conviction that solutions exist and can be discovered through methodical, persistent effort.

Toxic Positivity: Why It's Actually Workplace Poison

"Just stay positive!" chirps your coworker as your team faces another failed project launch. "Everything happens for a reason!"

These hollow encouragements aren't just unhelpful; they're examples of toxic positivity that can damage team morale and hinder real progress. While well intentioned, this "good vibes only" approach masks problems instead of solving them.

(continued)

(continued)

True optimism isn't about denying reality or suppressing negative emotions. It's about maintaining belief in your ability to improve situations while acknowledging current challenges. A genuine optimist doesn't ignore the failed launch—they analyze what went wrong while believing in the team's ability to succeed next time.

The key difference? Action. Where toxic positivity avoids problems, optimism faces them head-on. An optimistic leader doesn't just believe things will get better; they roll up their sleeves and make it happen. They combine hope with strategy, confidence with competence.

This bias toward action separates the true optimists. The optimist doesn't just say, "We'll figure something out"—they start mapping potential solutions immediately. They don't simply hope for improvement; they initiate the improvement process. When an optimistic product manager faces a critical bug before launch, they don't minimize it with "No worries, it'll be fine!" Instead, they acknowledge the challenge while simultaneously activating their problem-solving network: "This is a serious issue. Let's identify three potential approaches in the next hour and decide on our path forward."

Five Strategies for Being More Optimistic at Work

It's not easy to be an optimist, especially if you're surrounded by pessimists. Here's the truth: Tearing things down is infinitely easier than building them up. Any mid-level critic can poke holes in a new idea within seconds, listing all the reasons why something won't work. It requires zero creativity, minimal risk, and almost no intellectual investment. That's why pessimism feels so safe—it's the path of least resistance.

It also doesn't help move things forward. If you want to be successful, you have to address problems and find solutions. Optimism offers many strategies that lead to action and generate the success that will buoy your optimism.

1. The Quiet Power of Genuine Enthusiasm

I've spent years studying enthusiasm across organizations, and I've discovered that genuine enthusiasm isn't just a pleasant workplace bonus—it's the hidden engine of optimism and ultimately our happiness at work. But here's the challenge: You can't fake it. Genuine enthusiasm must be . . . well, genuine.

So how do you find and cultivate real enthusiasm, especially when your workday has begun to feel like Groundhog Day? Through my research, I've identified practices that consistently reignite genuine workplace enthusiasm.

Find the Work You Love and Do That Work Every Day

"Month-end closing is killing me," Kelsey sighed during our coaching session. "Almost two weeks of pure drudgery, twelve times a year." As a financial controller, she looked completely drained by her work.

But when she mentioned international reconciliations, something shifted. Her eyes lit up. "Actually, that part is fascinating. We have operations in 17 countries with different banking systems. Last month I found a pattern in our Malaysian transactions nobody else caught."

"That's the work you love," I explained. "You've discovered the specific aspect of your job that genuinely excites you—where time vanishes because what you're doing aligns perfectly with what energizes you."

This realization transformed her approach. Kelsey reorganized her workflow to begin each closing cycle with international reconciliations and negotiated with her boss to take on more global financial analysis throughout the month. By increasing the percentage of time spent on work she genuinely loved, her entire relationship with her job transformed.

"It's not about finding a different job," she told me later. "It's about finding the parts of your current job that you love and figuring out how to do more of them. That's been the key to my optimism— I'm no longer just enduring work; I've found my fuel."

Use Enthusiasm as Your Bridge to Optimism

When Julie's team faced a devastating setback—losing their biggest client—collective morale plummeted. During our emergency coaching session, I asked her a question that changed their trajectory: "What aspect of rebuilding genuinely interests you?"

After reflection, she identified that finding new work—researching and connecting with new potential clients—had always energized her. Rather than forcing herself to feel optimistic about their situation, she channeled her authentic enthusiasm for business development into action.

"I can't honestly say I feel optimistic about replacing the revenue yet," she told her team, "but I'm genuinely excited about some of these new companies I've identified. Their challenges align perfectly with our strengths."

By focusing first on what genuinely energized her, Julie created what I call an "enthusiasm bridge" to optimism.

This is the relationship between enthusiasm and optimism: Enthusiasm provides the energy to discover solutions, while optimism provides the belief that solutions exist. Together, they form a resilience loop that can carry you through the most daunting challenges.

Try this yourself: When facing a situation where optimism feels forced, ask, "What one aspect of this challenge genuinely interests me?"

Use that authentic interest—however small—as your entry point. Let your natural enthusiasm for that piece pull you toward broader optimism about the whole.

Yes, You Should Stop and Smell the Roses

Ever notice how we're like problem-seeking missiles at work? There's a reason for that! Our brains actually devote more neural real estate to spotting threats than good stuff. That ancient wiring kept our ancestors alive, but in today's workplace it can make us miss the little moments that bring joy.

Think about it: When was the last time you really savored something at work? That first sip of coffee that was just perfect, a "nice job" from your boss, or even just that quiet satisfaction when you finally solve a tricky problem? When we take time to really enjoy these moments, something amazing happens in our brains. Those feel-good chemicals—dopamine and serotonin—start flowing, and they don't just make us feel good now; they're actually creating pathways that make it easier to feel good later.

It's like training a joy muscle! By deliberately "scanning for joy"—actively looking for those bright spots in your day—you're pushing back against that negativity bias we all carry around. The cool part? The more you practice savoring, the better your brain gets at spotting the good stuff automatically.

And here's the best part: Savoring doesn't cost a thing and doesn't take extra time. It's just about tuning your attention to what's already there. When you make this a habit, you're not just changing your mood—you're literally changing how your brain perceives your work life. Pretty powerful stuff for something as simple as pausing to enjoy a moment, right?

---

2. The Gift of Surprise Gratitude

Expressing gratitude builds optimism because it makes *both people* (the giver of gratitude and the receiver) feel good. To really pack a punch, expressing gratitude should include two things: specificity and good timing.

Most of us offer generic expressions of gratitude, like thanking people for their help or support. But if you can be specific and talk about *how* someone helped you, and how it made you feel, that is gratitude that is really going to land. Try something like "Thank you for saying how my research reflected what you're seeing. I thought people might not agree with that and it really made me feel appreciated." This message is really clear about how the person helped you.

Great leaders surprise employees by expressing gratitude when they don't expect it, like offering an unsolicited compliment during a hallway encounter or writing a thank-you note that shares glowing customer feedback. Our brains are suspicious of planned events but are delighted by random acts of kindness.

When we thank people out of the blue, it makes a bigger impact—I call these "unexpected gratitude moments." Like a pleasant surprise appearing when least expected, unplanned appreciation catches people off guard. They're not waiting for praise, which makes it hit harder.

Here's what makes these surprise moments so powerful:

- **They feel more authentic.** When someone stops you in the hallway to share specific praise about a project you completed last week, your brain registers this as a genuine appreciation rather than an obligatory recognition.

- **They create "peak moments."** These are memorable experiences that stand out in our minds. A handwritten note appearing on your desk sharing customer feedback feels more meaningful than receiving the same feedback during a scheduled review meeting.

- **They fight "gratitude fatigue."** Regular, scheduled recognition can start to feel routine and lose its emotional impact. The element of surprise keeps appreciation fresh and meaningful.

3. Turn Your Worst Rejection into Your Greatest Comeback

When Beth received that "Re: Your Proposal" email, her heart sank. Six months of work dismissed in a politely worded rejection.

Instead of offering platitudes about doors closing and windows opening, I asked what the rejection actually said. The email mentioned their direction had "evolved considerably" and they were now "prioritizing scalability over immediate market impact."

"That's actually specific feedback," I pointed out. "Most rejections are vague. This one has breadcrumbs."

Beth rebuilt her proposal from scratch, emphasizing their scalable growth platform instead of her original market impact campaign. She titled it "Plan B: Scalability First" and framed it as an alternative approach based on their feedback.

Two weeks later, the client accepted her revised proposal and increased the budget by 30 percent. "Apparently, I'm the only vendor who 'truly understood their evolving needs,'" she laughed.

This isn't about positive thinking. Beth took a rejection, examined it differently, and found actionable information hiding in plain sight. Psychologists call this cognitive reframing. I call it professional survival.

Next time you face rejection, try this three-step process:

1. Get specific about exactly what didn't work (not just how you feel about it).

2. Look for information or opportunities that weren't visible before.

3. Make one concrete move based on this new perspective.

That last step is crucial. Reframing without action is just daydreaming.

When You Can't Shake Negativity

One of the things I've struggled with is that I get stuck in the negative. Like *really* stuck—the bad stuff sticks with me, while wins I wanted so badly just roll off my back.

Over the years, I've tried a lot of things to get me unstuck. The most dependable tool is a "joy journal"—it will almost always snap me out of my funk.

Every night before you go to sleep, write down three things that brought you joy that day and why. They don't have to be big things. It can be that great sandwich you had for lunch or that annoying meeting that got canceled.

What I love most about the joy journal is that it is a really sneaky way to shift your mindset. By writing down those three things that brought you joy, you are working against your hardwired negativity bias. And what you will find yourself doing is scanning for joy throughout the day. Now you are literally looking for the good moments because you know you have to write that in your joy journal. Do this every night for two weeks and you will start to feel happier.

In a seminal 2005 study, Seligman, Steen, Park, and Peterson tested several positive psychology interventions. Their "three good things" exercise (where participants wrote down three things that went well each day, and their causes, for one week) showed significant improvements in happiness and decreases in depressive symptoms. What's particularly interesting is that these benefits were still there six months later.[7]

---

4. Own Your Work, Own Your Future: The Autonomy-Optimism Connection

"I feel like I'm just a cog in a machine," Elena confessed during our first coaching session. As a talented marketing strategist at a global firm, she was drowning in other people's procedures and approvals. "I've got all these ideas, but I'm not allowed to implement any of them without running them through five layers of bureaucracy first."

Her eyes had lost their spark. Her voice had flattened. Classic signs of someone who feels powerless in their own career.

Six months later, I barely recognized her when we met for coffee. The transformation was dramatic—Elena radiated energy and excitement.

"What changed?" I asked.

"I have my own client now," she grinned. "The CEO liked my pitch so much, he gave me complete autonomy to handle their account my way."

Elena's story illustrates something I've seen repeatedly: Autonomy and optimism are intimately connected. When we feel in control of our work, optimism flourishes naturally. When we don't, even the sunniest disposition eventually clouds over.

This connection between having control and feeling hopeful isn't just coincidence—it's how our brains are wired. When we can actually influence our workday, we start seeing possibilities where we once saw problems.

Picture two scenarios: In one, you're following someone else's rigid instructions with zero flexibility. In the other, you're trusted to figure out the best approach. Which version of you feels more optimistic about the project's success?

That's what happened with Elena. When her company gave her real decision-making power, she stopped dreading challenges and started seeing them as puzzles she could solve. Her "I've got this" attitude grew directly from having actual influence over her work.

I've watched this pattern play out countless times. When people feel like passive passengers in their work lives, even natural optimists eventually burn out. But give those same people meaningful control, and their outlook transforms—often within weeks.

The takeaway? If you want optimism to flourish in your team, autonomy isn't just a nice perk—it's essential fuel.

5. Visualize Success: The Olympic Secret That Works in the Boardroom

"I bombed my last presentation," Franklin told me, slumping in his chair. "And now I have to present to the entire executive team next week. I'm already having nightmares about it."

"Let's try something different this time," I suggested. "Instead of rehearsing the failure, let's rehearse the success."

Looking skeptical, Franklin closed his eyes as I guided him through a detailed visualization exercise. I had him imagine everything—the room, the faces of the executives, the feeling of confidence as he answered challenging questions, the sound of applause when he finished, the congratulatory messages afterward.

"Do this for five minutes every morning and evening until your presentation," I told him. "Your brain doesn't distinguish clearly between a vividly imagined experience and reality."

A week later, Franklin couldn't stop smiling when we met. "I nailed it," he said. "It felt familiar, like I'd already been there before."

What Franklin experienced wasn't magic—it was the same technique that elite athletes have relied on for decades. Michael Phelps, the most decorated Olympian of all time, would visualize his races in such detail that he could tell you exactly how many strokes he would take between each wall of the pool. His coach, Bob Bowman, had him visualize perfect races and also problematic ones where he had to overcome obstacles—like the time his goggles actually did fill with water during the 2008 Olympic final, just as he had visualized. Despite swimming blind for nearly the entire race, he won gold and set a world record because he had mentally rehearsed that exact scenario.[8]

When you visualize an action, your brain fires many of the same neural circuits that activate when you're actually performing that action.[9] It's like installing and testing software before you need to run it in a critical situation.

To harness this power yourself, try mental rehearsal. Before high-stakes events like job interviews or crucial negotiations, walk yourself through each moment in exquisite detail. Imagine entering the room, shaking hands, answering difficult questions with confidence, and concluding successfully. Practice this repeatedly until it feels natural.

Visualization won't magically make things happen—you still have to do the work. But it prepares your mind to recognize opportunities, remain calm under pressure, and approach challenges with confidence. It's like programming your GPS for success before starting the journey.

Building a Culture of Practical Optimism

I witnessed a remarkable transformation with a large healthcare organization I worked with a few years ago. It was a hospital system struggling with burnout and high turnover. Their new CEO didn't just talk about optimism—she systematically rebuilt the culture around it.

First, she focused on psychological safety. "We can't solve problems we can't discuss," she told the leadership team. She instituted a "no-blame" reporting system for errors and near-misses, emphasizing learning over punishment. Within months, reported incidents increased dramatically—not because more errors were occurring, but because staff felt safe highlighting problems.

Next, she modeled positive leadership. She banned "yes, but" thinking in meetings, replacing it with "yes, and" to build on ideas rather than shutting them down. She demonstrated active listening, maintained eye contact during conversations, and implemented a "good-news start" policy where meetings began with successes before tackling challenges.

Most powerfully, she invested in learning. "Healthcare is always advancing," she told staff. "If we're not growing, we're falling behind." She allocated 5 percent of work hours for professional development and created a generous education reimbursement program. Suddenly, nurses and doctors who had been thinking about leaving were planning their futures instead.

Finally, she restructured workflows to increase autonomy. Each unit received clear outcomes they needed to achieve, but had significant freedom in how to reach those goals. Teams could customize their approaches based on their unique patient populations and staff strengths.

When these elements combine, they create powerful organizational optimism that becomes self-reinforcing. Teams believe they can overcome challenges, so they persist longer, collaborate more effectively, and ultimately achieve more ambitious goals.

As Antoine de Saint-Exupéry, the author of *The Little Prince*, said (and Netflix quotes on their culture page): "If you want to build a ship, don't drum up the people to gather wood, divide the work, and give orders. Instead, teach them to yearn for the vast and endless sea."

This is the essence of building optimism into your culture—helping people see possibilities where others see only problems, and giving them the safety, leadership, learning, and autonomy they need to turn those possibilities into reality.

What all these examples—from NASA and *Star Wars* to struggling schools and overloaded emergency rooms—demonstrate is that practical optimism isn't just positive thinking. It's a deliberate approach to challenges that combines clear-eyed assessment of reality with an unwavering belief in our capacity to improve that reality through creative problem-solving, perseverance, and strategic action.

The Happiness, Works Method: Optimism

- **Spark genuine enthusiasm** by finding what naturally energizes you at work. Just like Kelsey changed how she felt about her job by making it possible to do more of what she loved, you can boost optimism by leaning into your authentic passions.

- **Show gratitude when people don't expect it** to really pack a punch. Catching people off-guard with praise is effective because it feels more authentic, creates peak moments, and fights "gratitude fatigue."

- **Reframe obstacles into opportunities** with one powerful question: "How might this challenge actually be opening a door I couldn't see before?" When Beth dug into the feedback she received and used it to find a way to try again, she turned defeat into a huge success.

- **Focus your energy where you have control.** When Elena gained autonomy over her work—and control over the output—her optimism blossomed.

- **Visualize your way through obstacles** by mentally rehearsing both success and potential problems. Before his Olympic race, Michael Phelps had already practiced "swimming blind" hundreds of times in his mind. When his goggles actually filled with water, it felt familiar rather than catastrophic.

- **Build optimism into your team's DNA** by celebrating problem-solving rather than perfect execution. NASA didn't succeed because everything went right—they succeeded because their culture transformed "failure is not an option" from a slogan into a mindset that turned disasters into triumphs.

151

Chapter 8

Putting Happiness into Action

I've spent years in the trenches coaching all kinds of people through their darkest workplace moments, and I've discovered something eye-opening: While good intentions matter, it's what you actually do that transforms your experience.

Here's the thing that keeps me up at night: I spend my days listening to people tell me why they are unhappy at work, about what they hate about work, about what's not working about work, and I've watched certain situations pop up again and again like clockwork.

They're so common that I think of them as the Seven Deadly Setbacks that derail people's happiness at work. They're the silent happiness killers that can turn your dream job into a nightmare. If you're nodding your head right now, you've probably faced at least one of these career-crushing moments.

Get ready to dive deep. I'm about to take you behind the scenes of my coaching practice, sharing real stories (with names changed, of course) that will probably feel eerily familiar. For each setback, we'll explore not just what went wrong, but how to fight back using our happiness framework in Chapters 3–7. Better yet, I'll show you exactly how to measure your progress as you bounce back.

This isn't about theory anymore—we're way past that. Think of this chapter as your battlefield guide to protecting your happiness when everything hits the fan. By the time we're done, these setbacks won't stand a chance against your new arsenal of practical tools. Instead of letting these challenges derail you for weeks, you'll know exactly how to get back on track, rebuild your momentum, and keep those happiness-building habits strong.

Ready to turn those career-crushing moments into mere speed bumps? Let's dive in.

Setback 1: You Hate Your Coworker; Now What?

"Help! I hate my office enemy!"

Let's talk about something we all deal with eventually: not getting along with a manager, a supervisor, a coworker, or a colleague. It's awkward, it's draining, and it makes work miserable. But here's the thing: Avoiding the issue doesn't help. Unresolved conflict at work can tank your happiness *and* it can destroy your team's performance.

We've all been there: that moment when you realize you and someone at work are like oil and water. Whether it's your manager, your teammate, or that person from accounting, workplace conflict is more than just uncomfortable. It can undermine productivity, damage relationships, and create a ripple effect of negativity throughout the organization.

Let me tell you about Lauren's situation. She was crushing it at a Fortune 500 company when she hit a major roadblock—a senior manager who seemed to be on a mission to make Lauren's life difficult. We're talking full hostile mode: public takedowns in meetings, screaming matches, and the kind of aggressive avoidance that makes middle school drama look mature. Lauren was at her wits' end, completely baffled by the hostility and desperate for solutions. It got so bad that Lauren finally snapped, storming out of a meeting in what she hoped was a powerful statement . . . but felt more like a desperate escape. (Spoiler alert: There's a much better way to handle this.)

What to Do

The conflict was at a stalemate, but I walked Lauren through what she should do next.

Step 1: Cool Off

The good thing about storming out of a meeting (which I would never normally recommend) is that it lets you distance yourself from the situation—literally. Before Lauren could start working on a solution, she needed to get her emotions in check and cool off. If she didn't, the conflict would undoubtedly escalate.

Remember that moment when you're about to send a fiery email and your inner voice screams "*Wait!*"? Listen to that voice. Lauren's dramatic exit actually gave her one gift—breathing room. Instead of plotting revenge, she took a walk. And then she did something I advise all of my clients to do in the heat of the moment: brain-dumping everything onto paper.

Writing down your thoughts helps you stop replaying that mental movie of what you should've said. I asked Lauren to write down answers to these questions: What happened right before this woman started yelling at Lauren? What seemed to upset her so much? What feelings did this bring up for Lauren?

Step 2: Get Curious and Reframe

Lauren explained that she grew up in a household with a lot of yelling, so being yelled at is a trigger for a lot of feelings. It's hard to feel resilient in those moments, but my coaching practice has made me realize that people have triggers like this. What has helped my clients is one of psychology's great insights: Most of the time, when dealing with other people, we assume that people's behavior is *who they are*, rather than what they're dealing with.[1]

Let me explain. It's called the "fundamental attribution error" and we're all guilty of this mental shortcut. We jump to label someone's character based on their actions, while overlooking the circumstances that might be driving their behavior. What the "fundamental attribution error" tells us is that we tend to think people are just jerks rather than considering that they might be dealing with their own mess. Maybe your boss isn't actually out to get you; maybe they're drowning in their own stress. And this means that it's crucial to ask questions and analyze what's really going on.

When Lauren's colleague snapped at her during a presentation, her first instinct was to file them away under "hopelessly difficult." But by resisting that reflexive judgment and getting curious instead, she could start a conversation with them. Through this dialogue, she discovered they were wrestling with an overloaded schedule and a family crisis. That insight shifted everything, transforming what could have been a permanent rift into a discussion about how they could better support each other.

This mindset change helps you approach your situation with curiosity rather than blame. In Lauren's case, it showed her how to approach having a conversation with the person who just yelled at her and gave her a strategy for how they could move forward.

Step 3: Start a Conversation (Without Blame)

My advice to Lauren (and to all of my clients) was that she needed to have a plan going into this conversation. She needed to have a goal for the outcome. Knowing exactly what you want to achieve before starting a conversation will shape everything that follows. It's unlikely that you'll become best friends with this person you're in conflict with, but can you learn to work together and treat each other with respect? Or do you simply want to give them feedback and make them understand the distress that the situation is causing you?

In Lauren's case, she wanted a better working relationship. This meant establishing a shared goal: When Lauren initiated the conversation, she did it by saying, "I'd really like us to get on the same page because I think we both want this project to go smoothly." She made sure to approach her privately, rather than risk clashing in public.

Lauren pulled off something pretty impressive: She approached her work nemesis with a common goal. Genius move. No accusations, no "you always" statements, just a focus on shared goals. It's workplace diplomacy 101.

Sometimes the smallest changes create the biggest shifts. Lauren and her boss started with one simple rule: no more raised voices. Baby steps, people.

Here's the truth: You don't need to be best friends with everyone at work. (Thank goodness, right?) But learning to navigate these tricky relationships? That's your ticket to actually enjoying work again.

It's also important to realize that there's no such thing as winning in these conversations. And that's a critically important mindset shift. Proving that you're more right than the other person, or that they should feel bad, is not going to get you anywhere (even if it might feel good for a moment). Instead, focus on listening and learning, and use what you hear to create a goal that you both can work toward.

Success Metrics

For Lauren, success was coming up with a solution that allowed her to move on and refocus on enjoying her work again. They agreed to start small, by looking together for one small change that would make it easier for them to get along.

The key is to keep building on these small changes until you feel the obstacle is behind you. Don't just make a small change and leave it there. Set a time to follow up (for example, "Let's touch base in a couple of weeks and see how things are going") and start to build your progress loop by coming up with another small change.

Think of it this way: Workplace happiness isn't about having zero problems; it's about learning how to handle problems when they happen. Ready to try your hand at workplace diplomacy? You might be surprised at how much a little curiosity and conversation can shift things.

Framework Fundamentals for Lauren

Lauren succeeded by applying different parts of the happiness framework:

- **Resilience (see Chapter 4):** Reframing is a strategy that changes stress from a blocker to a sign that we need to take action.

- **Trust (see Chapter 5):** By getting curious about her colleague's defensiveness, she was able to break the cycle and start rebuilding their relationship.

- **Progress (see Chapter 6):** By starting with a "micro-habit" (no more raised voices), Lauren and her colleague could start building up small wins.

Setback 2: Navigating a Toxic Work Environment?

It's possible to imagine changing one person, but what do you do when the whole environment needs to change?

One toxic leader can poison an entire workplace, something my client Zahra discovered the hard way. As a director at a large ad agency, she should have been living her dream job. Instead, she found herself dreading each workday, all because of her boss, Mark.

Mark was the kind of vice president who built his success on others' foundations while claiming he'd laid every brick himself. He moved through the office like a black hole of attention—every conversation had to orbit around his problems, his priorities, his demands. When things didn't go his way, his anger rippled through the department, leaving anxiety in its wake.

Soon, the office culture warped to survive in Mark's shadow. Zahra watched as talented colleagues transformed into sycophants, stepping on each other in their scramble to curry Mark's favor. Those who tried to maintain their integrity found themselves increasingly isolated.

Despite loving everything else about her role—the challenges, her team, the work itself—Zahra found herself dreaming of a new job, wondering if it was time to walk away.

What to Do

Zahra needed a little bit of strategic optimism.

The key is to focus on what you can control, carving out spaces for yourself that are free of toxicity. Maybe you block off periods of uninterrupted time for work where you don't look at messages. For Zahra, who ran her own team, she worked hard to protect her people from outside toxic influences and create and cultivate a healthy, optimistic culture for them.

Reclaim Your Personal Power

Part of feeling in control is asserting your reality, rather than letting someone like Mark have that power. When someone else controls the narrative of your work life, you start to lose yourself. But you can take that power back, one small act at a time.

Strategic optimism isn't about pasting on a smile—it's about finding pockets of possibility even in toxic terrain. It means deliberately seeking out and creating spaces where you can thrive, despite the challenges around you.

For Zahra, this meant turning her team into an oasis. While she couldn't control Mark's behavior, she could shield her people from his toxicity, fostering an environment where creativity and collaboration flourished. She carved out "deep work" periods where notifications went dark and real progress could happen. These weren't just productivity tactics: They were survival strategies that kept her professional spirit alive.

Here are some ways to practice strategic optimism in a challenging workplace:

- Create "micro-environments" of positivity by establishing regular coffee chats with supportive colleagues.

- Design your workspace to spark joy, whether that's through photos, plants, or inspiring quotes.

- Schedule regular "wins reviews" where you and your team celebrate small victories.

- Build alliances with other departments, creating a network of mutual support.

- Set aside time each week for projects that energize you, even if they're small.

- Mentor others, turning your challenges into learning opportunities for colleagues.

The key is recognizing that while you can't control the whole ecosystem, you can cultivate your own corner of it. This isn't just about survival—it's about refusing to let someone else's toxicity define your professional story. Each small act of optimism is a step toward reclaiming your workplace narrative and rebuilding your sense of agency.

Get Strategic About How You Respond

Just like with visualization exercises, you can plan out how you'll react to difficult situations in advance. For example, Zahra wrote scripts for difficult conversations that happened (such as when Mark tried to take credit for her team's work) and practiced how she would respond.

As she built up relationships in her department, she found allies who could speak up on her behalf and developed a support network she could talk with about her problems. (It turned out that many of them understood all too well.) She found a mentor outside of the organization who gave her good insights and acted as a "pressure release" system (reminding her that she was not the problem).

She also worked on reframing challenging interactions as opportunities to demonstrate leadership. When Mark interrupted her in meetings, she had more than a prepared response—she had a vision for how these moments could strengthen her reputation for grace under pressure. She might reply, "Thanks for that perspective, Mark. Now, let me build on that idea. ... " She turned what could have been confrontations into collaborations, each interaction reinforcing her role as a bridge-builder.

This approach is about actively creating positive outcomes even in tough situations. When you've already imagined how to transform difficult moments into constructive exchanges, you maintain your optimism and keep sight of the bigger picture: your growth, your impact, and your future success.

By preparing for challenges with hope rather than dread, you're crafting opportunities for small wins that build toward larger victories. Each positive interaction becomes proof that you can shape your professional story, regardless of the circumstances around you.

Focus on Your Professional Development

"Future-casting" is imagining positive scenarios for yourself and working toward them. By building up your own abilities, and your presence, you gain more power to influence your colleagues. By developing your skills and networking within your industry, you'll grow your reputation and earn yourself more autonomy.

Zahra wanted to learn how to give more persuasive presentations, so people would be more likely to follow her approach (rather than Mark's). She started by imagining what her ideal presentation would look like and working backward to see what steps she needed to take to achieve it.

Zahra also wanted her team to be ready for their next big opportunity. She called an hour-long meeting where she asked everyone to polish their crystal ball and try to predict what their team's next opportunities might look like—and how they could position themselves to take advantage of them. This helped her team feel like they were steering their own ship, rather than letting Mark set the course.

None of us can predict the future precisely, but taking steps to prepare for the most likely outcomes—and being ready for them—means that you're moving toward where the puck is going, rather than getting trapped in your current crisis.

Master Your Mindset

It can help to think of a toxic situation as a test of your resilience. Remember the principles of post-traumatic growth—that adversity can make you stronger—and use the difficult situation as a springboard to finding new ways to succeed.

Zahra reframed her situation as a learning opportunity, an inevitable obstacle on the path to success that she was excited to learn how to overcome. She started to mentor junior people who were struggling, which gave her a sense of meaning and purpose.

By focusing on what she could control—and how these trials could make her stronger—she found that Mark's energy didn't breach the walls of her watertight containers quite so easily.

Success Metrics

In Zahra's case, success was not defined by changing the toxic behavior of others (which is almost impossible), but by taking control of her workday to neutralize negative influences. She grew her professional network, which introduced more positive influences into her day-to-day work life. She thought more about her future and career direction, which made her realize that this toxicity was just a temporary obstacle. And she strengthened her work–life boundaries, so that the impact of unhelpful behavior was minimized.

When she did need to face toxic behavior, she reframed it as an opportunity to learn that would help her in the future. Learning how to manage toxicity gave her more confidence when faced with unfair criticism. And she took pride in strengthening her resilience, which gave her a feeling that the future she wanted was inevitable, since it was now much harder to knock her off track.

Framework Fundamentals for Zahra

In this scenario, Zahra was able to use:

- **Resilience (see Chapter 4):** By building out her support system, she no longer felt alone in her struggle.

- **Optimism (see Chapter 7):** By visualizing success and future-casting, she was able to regain control over her environment and team direction.

Setback 3: Dealing with a Big Failure

Everybody fails. Failure is an act, not a person. The happiest people realize that it's not the failure that's important, but what you do afterward.

Jeremy learned this truth the hard way. After years of hoping to work at one of the industry's most respected companies, he finally landed his dream role. But six months in, his big break had become his biggest nightmare. The project he was leading had spiraled—deadlines whooshed past, the budget hemorrhaged by 40 percent, and stakeholders watched their requirements vanish into the ether. Before he could right the ship, the executive team pulled the plug.

The aftermath was brutal. His leadership team's sideways glances spoke volumes about their faith in his abilities. Three team members, reading the writing on the wall, had already jumped ship to other departments. The confident leader who'd once strode into executive meetings now felt his heart race at the ping of a calendar invite.

"My reputation is in shreds," he confided during our coaching sessions, his voice heavy with the weight of lost confidence. "How do you rebuild trust when everyone's waiting for you to fail again?" The irony wasn't lost on him: The same self-assurance that had landed him this role now seemed as distant as his former success.

What to Do

We needed a plan for Jeremy to rebuild trust within the organization and feel like he was moving in the right direction again. After several deep coaching sessions, a path forward emerged. Rather than just hoping time would heal his reputation, we crafted a strategic comeback in four parts.

Step 1: Face the Music, Then Rewrite the Script

First, Jeremy needed to own the story of what went wrong—but own it with purpose. He conducted a thorough post-mortem that didn't just list failures, but extracted valuable lessons. Instead of letting others whisper about what happened, he took control of the narrative. He mapped out a communication strategy that turned his hard-earned insights into a blueprint for future success, sharing these findings in thoughtful one-on-ones with his team and key stakeholders.

From that analysis, he drew up a list of specific lessons for both himself and the company and made his recommendations for how these kinds of mistakes could be prevented in the future.

He also had to be proactive about sharing these findings. This meant drafting a communication plan for how he would broadcast these insights to different stakeholders. He then set up one-on-one meetings with people on his team to explain how they would be moving forward.

Step 2: Transform Failure into Fuel

To regain his confidence, Jeremy needed to look inward and be honest about what he needed to change. After confronting what went wrong, Jeremy turned his failure into a blueprint for growth. He mapped out a development plan that went beyond surface fixes, identifying specific skill gaps that had contributed to his project's collapse. While he pursued formal training in project management and leadership, his most valuable education came from leaders who had walked through similar fires. He set up one-on-one meetings to learn from those who walked in his shoes. Their hard-won wisdom helped him see his situation not as a career-ender, but as a powerful teaching moment.

Finally, he put his post-mortem into action by coming up with new risk management protocols so that he could adapt more quickly the next time things started to go wrong. He then transformed these lessons into practical safeguards, creating early warning systems for the exact issues that had blindsided him before. Each step wasn't just about recovery—it was about emerging as a stronger, more insightful leader than before.

Step 3: Rebuild Relationships

Jeremy knew that many people had lost trust in him, but he wanted to change that. He'd always thought of himself as someone with strong people skills, so he decided to put them to work and rebuild the damaged relationships he had with specific executives and people on his team. Jeremy leaned into his natural strength in building relationships, but with a new awareness.

This meant more frequent check-ins with team members and an emphasis on listening to their concerns. He knew that failure was easier to overcome if detected early, so he encouraged people to tell him when they thought something was going wrong and he embraced radical transparency in his status updates so that no one thought he was hiding bad news. (Just like Alan Mulally did with his traffic light system of reporting; see Chapter 5 for details.) He also began to ask for candid 360 feedback on his performance every quarter, so that he could address issues early and resolve them with the people concerned.

Step 4: Improve Your Own Resilience

The final piece was about making Jeremy himself more resilient. We worked to transform his stress response from a liability into an asset. He developed new coping strategies, from supporting others facing challenges (which paradoxically helped him) to maintaining strict boundaries between work and recovery time. He cultivated a network of trusted mentors and colleagues who could offer perspective when things got tough. Most importantly, he learned to practice self-compassion—understanding that setbacks are universal, and that growth comes not from endless self-criticism but from balanced self-reflection.

Each step built on the others, creating not just a recovery plan but a template for sustainable leadership. Jeremy wasn't just getting back to where he'd been; he was building something stronger.

Success Metrics

Recovering from a major failure doesn't happen overnight. For Jeremy, rebuilding started with small, achievable goals: the kind he could reach within three to six months. These weren't moonshots; they were modest victories that would help shift the narrative from "the failed project" to "the leader who's learning and adapting." At this stage, even subtle shifts in team dynamics mattered more than dramatic results.

While nurturing these quick wins, Jeremy also laid groundwork for larger victories. Instead of fixating on these longer-term metrics, he tracked small but meaningful indicators: more open discussions in team meetings, increased voluntary feedback, and growing participation in project planning.

Finally, Jeremy began to focus on his growth and leadership development as much as project outcomes. He believed that investing in himself would pay off with better results—especially because it would help him to recover the happiness he'd lost and move forward with renewed optimism. After all, the best measure of recovery isn't just reaching your old heights—it's discovering you can climb even higher.

Framework Fundamentals for Jeremy

Here's how Jeremy used the framework to get back on track:

- **Relationships (see Chapter 3):** Jeremy rebuilt his support circles to regain their trust and his belief in himself.

- **Resilience (see Chapter 4):** By being honest about what he needed to learn, he made himself better at withstanding future challenges. He also learned to lean on others in times of need.

- **Optimism (see Chapter 7):** By asserting his autonomy, he was able to see a way out of what seemed like an impossible situation and chart a course forward.

Setback 4: The Low-Trust Team

Trust is the invisible thread that holds teams together—until it snaps. Just ask Jackson, whose software development team was quietly imploding under the weight of broken trust.

As the team leader of six developers, Jackson watched a concerning pattern unfold. Knowledge became a closely guarded treasure. Setbacks turned into finger-pointing festivals. Team meetings morphed into exercises in defensive posturing, where valuable feedback withered in the face of crossed arms and clenched jaws. His developers began documenting everything—not to improve clarity, but to protect themselves from blame.

During a particularly candid coaching session, Jackson confronted a harsh reality: This erosion of trust was sabotaging their success. Project deadlines started slipping. Code quality suffered. Innovation stagnated. And now the final warning bell was tolling, as two of his star performers quietly polished their résumés. Despite his well-intentioned attempts at team building, Jackson knew that trust, once fractured, wouldn't be repaired by a few rounds of office trivia or trust falls. He faced a critical question: How could he rebuild the foundation of trust before his team, and their critical project, crumbled completely?

What to Do

You can't solve a problem until you understand it. While Jackson knew that a lack of trust was the problem, he didn't know why. To find out, he sent his entire team an anonymous survey about what was making it difficult for people to trust their teammates and then used the results to start a conversation about the challenges people were feeling.

One of the themes that came up was a lack of transparency—people were afraid to admit mistakes, which led to a culture of hiding them. Since the mistakes were hidden, people often didn't know who was responsible for them and the blame game would begin. People felt helpless because they had a hard time making progress when they couldn't trust the quality of the code.

Jackson realized that he had been focusing on making progress on the team's goals without paying enough attention to how they were achieved. He got the team to temporarily stop work on their project for three days and do a "bug hunt" (finding problems with the code) so the team could find and fix the biggest problems, rebuilding trust in the code quality. Afterward, he created a leaderboard for who found and fixed the most bugs going forward, making it clear that reporting errors would help the team ship a stronger product. To encourage collaboration, he set up weekly "pair programming" sessions where top performers would be paired with more junior programmers to write the code together, which simultaneously built trust and taught people how to avoid errors.

Jackson then got to work on team processes that would build trust even more. He asked everyone to document their decision-making processes and regularly share the outcomes with their teammates.

Putting Happiness into Action

He developed a "responsibility matrix" that better defined each person's role on the team. And he made his project allocation decisions more transparent by including his rationales for why each person was receiving that particular assignment.

He knew that things would improve only if *everyone* communicated better with one another, not just with him. He got the team to formalize their preferred communication methods so they were clear to each other. He also encouraged people to share more candid feedback, making it clear that the aim was to support one another and improve, rather than to point the finger. He asked people to propose experiments where it was "safe to fail" (but success would lead to big improvements). And he started to celebrate team successes at the beginning of their weekly meeting, highlighting small wins that reinvigorated the team's sense of progress.

Jackson also realized that he had to look in the mirror and start to share his own mistakes. He started by talking about his own failure to build a transparent culture for the team. He made it clear that he cared more about course corrections than who was at fault for mistakes. And he encouraged everyone to come to him anytime if they had concerns about the team's approach. He reinforced this message at his weekly one-on-ones with team members. Individual status updates were deemphasized; instead, Jackson asked people for their honest feedback on the team's performance.

Success Metrics

The immediate impacts were modest, but the long-term changes were monumental. Building trust takes time, but once it gets momentum, it can lead to a real transformation.

In the beginning, Jackson noticed that people were speaking more in team meetings and there was less blaming and defensiveness. Information started to flow more freely and a friendly competition developed over who could fix the most bugs.

After several months, the changes really started to become obvious. The team was moving faster and project completion rates were going up. It became harder to find bugs in the code, maybe because the top performers were now actively mentoring junior developers. Feedback from stakeholders was much improved and the team's reputation had changed so much that Jackson was now fielding requests from people to join the team.

On the HR team's annual survey, the team's scores for job satisfaction and feeling psychological safety were some of the highest at the company. Jackson himself had developed new confidence in his leadership skills and now really enjoyed the team's social functions.

Most importantly, Jackson has realized that the work of managing team culture never stops. Building trust is a gradual process that requires consistent effort and showing trustworthy behavior at all levels. Success is measured not just in improved metrics and business outcomes, but in the quality of relationships and the team's ability to effectively handle challenges together.

Framework Fundamentals for Jackson

Jackson used several trust tactics (see Chapter 5) to turn around his team:

- **Make failure visible:** By improving transparency in decision-making and processes, Jackson gave his team permission to trust again.

- **Candor:** By encouraging candor, he allowed his team to rebuild trust and created pathways for improvement.

- **Vulnerability:** By demonstrating his commitment to change, and admitting his own mistakes, he made it easier for his team to follow his example.

171

Setback 5: The Paradox of Drowning in Success

Kim was the office superstar, the go-to problem-solver who never said no. When two colleagues departed, leadership saw an obvious solution—hand their work to Kim. She'd make it work. She always did.

But three months later, Kim's carefully constructed world was cracking. The headaches came first, pounding reminders that she hadn't slept properly in weeks. Then the anxiety attacks started, stealing her breath during late-night email sessions that had become her new normal. Her family dinners had transformed into a symphony of notification pings and hurried responses to "urgent" messages.

At work, the cracks were widening. Deadlines, once sacred to her, began slipping through her fingers. Meeting discussions floated past her like background noise as she struggled to focus through the fog of exhaustion. The creative spark that had once made her invaluable now felt like a distant memory. Her legendary patience had worn so thin that she found herself snapping at colleagues over minor issues.

The bitter irony wasn't lost on her: The very excellence that had made her indispensable was now threatening everything she'd built. She still loved her job, but as she sat in her office late one evening, staring at an endless to-do list, a chilling thought crossed her mind: Was she watching her career and health burn out in real time?

What to Do

When your house is on fire, you have to put out the fire.

Embracing this principle of immediate intervention, Kim's first move was to stop the blaze of burnout from consuming her completely. She drew hard lines in the sand for when she could work (no more emails at dinner or working into the wee hours) and asked her colleagues to keep communication to normal work hours. She conducted a brutal audit of her workload, separating the essential from the expendable. She crafted her "stress survival guide"—a personal playbook that distinguished between red flags and challenges she could reframe as opportunities.

The second step was realizing that, when the workload couldn't be reduced, it could be optimized. Using her workload audit, Kim mapped every responsibility against the time it truly required (not the compressed timeline she'd been forcing herself to meet). Then she channeled her inner minimalist, ruthlessly pruning tasks that could be delegated to her team or eliminated entirely. For what remained, she set realistic deadlines that wouldn't require superhuman effort.

The next step demanded that Kim turn into more of a diplomat. She documented her capacity issues and their ripple effects on both her work quality and her health, presenting this evidence to her manager. Instead of hiding problems from her manager, she put her trust in her—asking for her help in managing the workload and her support for setting boundaries. Likewise, she was honest with her team about her limitations and asked for their patience and a helping hand.

Her calendar became her stronghold: Breaks were no longer optional luxuries but scheduled necessities. She carved out sacred morning hours for "deep work" when her mind was sharpest. To seal the boundary between work and life, Kim developed her "shutdown ritual"—a daily practice of reviewing tomorrow's tasks and tidying her workspace that signaled to her brain that work time was truly over. Work notifications were banished from her phone, and auto-responses stood guard against after-hours email intrusions.

The last item on our list was the hardest—learning to say "no" or "not now" (which is even more effective) to new requests. While this made her profoundly uncomfortable, she spoke with a mentor and did a little research on how to do this effectively. She then wrote down some scripts she could follow so that she didn't just default to saying yes.

The long game became Kim's final focus. Exercise sessions were marked in her calendar with the same weight as client meetings. She rekindled both her work and nonwork friendships through weekly meetups and discovered a new passion in art classes. Knowing her tendency to backslide into old habits, she enlisted her inner circle as accountability partners, asking them to be the guardrails she needed to stay on her path to recovery.

Success Metrics

All of these steps were designed to give Kim a feeling of control over her life and gradually reduce her stress levels.

The first sign of success, which happened within a few weeks, was cutting out overtime (almost) entirely. She also started sleeping better and having fewer headaches and anxiety attacks. She slowly became less guilty about taking breaks.

After a couple of months, she felt like she'd achieved a "new normal." She was sticking to her new schedule and felt like she was delivering better work. There was still a lot to do, but prioritizing and delegating meant that the important things always got done. She no longer felt like she was taking out her stress on her colleagues.

Six months later, Kim had rediscovered the spark that first drew her to her work. Her manager's feedback glowed with praise, but the real victory was more personal: She could sit through family dinner without her mind drifting to unfinished tasks. The headaches had vanished, replaced by the familiar rush of tackling challenging projects—this time without the crushing weight of feeling overwhelmed. Her reputation wasn't just intact; it had grown stronger. She'd become known as someone who delivered excellence while modeling sustainable success, opening doors for her next career move.

The journey had taught her something profound: Mastering stress wasn't about dimming her light; it was about learning to burn bright without burning out. She'd discovered that peak performance and personal well-being weren't opposing forces, but rather two sides of the same coin. True success, she realized, wasn't just about surviving the storm, but learning to dance in the rain.

Framework Fundamentals for Kim

Kim was able to regain control of her work life using:

- **Relationships (see Chapter 3):** Kim realized she couldn't solve this problem on her own, but leaned on the support of her manager and colleagues.
- **Resilience (see Chapter 4):** By getting serious about self-care, she rediscovered what had made her such a superstar in the first place.

Setback 6: When You're Stuck in Career Quicksand

Another morning, another LinkedIn notification celebrating someone else's career leap. That's where Malka found herself, five years into a marketing role that had slowly transformed from exciting to suffocating. On paper, everything looked fine: steady performance reviews, reliable raises, solid benefits. But beneath that comfortable surface, her enthusiasm had flatlined. Each Monday morning arrived like a weight, while her LinkedIn feed had become a carousel of other people's progress, feeding a growing sense of being left behind.

During a vulnerable coaching session, Malka admitted what she'd been afraid to voice: She was "slowly dying" professionally. While her friends celebrated career leaps, she felt anchored by golden handcuffs—that seductive combination of comfortable salary and familiar routine that makes change feel simultaneously urgent and impossible.

What to Do

What Malka discovered was an enthusiasm deficit. The spark that once lit up her Monday mornings had dimmed to a flicker. Like many professionals, she'd fallen into the trap of confusing competence with fulfillment. Yes, she could manage social media campaigns in her sleep, but that wasn't the same as waking up excited to do it.

The journey back to engagement started with brutal honesty. Through systematic self-assessment, she mapped out her skills, interests, and frustrations. A pattern emerged: Her passion wasn't in the tactical world of social media but in the strategic realm of brand storytelling. She realized she lit up when talking about crafting compelling narratives that connect with people. Her eyes brightened when discussing visual aesthetics and messaging architecture. These were clues to what could reignite her professional passion.

Rather than making an immediate leap, Malka took calculated steps to build momentum. She volunteered for brand-focused projects at work and helped a friend reimagine her candle business's brand identity. Each small win strengthened her confidence and provided real-world experience in her target field. Working on these projects was a chance to lose herself in the kind of work that made time disappear. She found herself sketching brand concepts during lunch breaks, reading industry blogs for pleasure, and actually looking forward to testing new approaches.

The turning point came when Malka started actively cultivating professional connections. She joined her industry's professional association, not just as a member but as an active participant hungry for knowledge. The annual conference became her launching pad—she had dozens of conversations with brand managers who'd made similar transitions and could provide both practical insights and emotional support. These connections created a psychological safety net, making the prospect of change feel less daunting.

Success Metrics

As her network grew and her skills expanded, Malka's enthusiasm naturally rekindled. She still faced fears—Would she have to start over? Take a pay cut? Fail completely?—but now she had the support system to process these concerns productively. Each informational interview and project success built trust in her ability to navigate the transition.

Ironically, Malka's journey led her right back to her current company, but in a completely different role. When a brand management position opened up, her newly developed skills and internal relationships made her the natural choice. But the real victory was the rekindled sense of possibility and progress that had vanished from her professional life.

Her story reveals a crucial truth: Escaping career stagnation isn't always about changing your title. Sometimes it's about rediscovering your enthusiasm, building resilience, and creating connections that make growth possible. The external change matters less than the internal transformation—from stuck to unstoppable, from isolated to connected, from stagnant to growing. That's the kind of progress that brings sustainable happiness back to your work life.

Setback 7: When You Don't Have a Best Friend at Work

How to make more friends at work is the most common question I'm asked—by a mile. This simple question often draws nervous laughter or a wistful sigh. And no wonder—a staggering 80 percent of people say they don't have a best friend at their workplace.[2] Behind this statistic lies a deeper story about workplace happiness and success.

When Jordan first came to me for coaching, he confided that despite his professional success, something vital was missing from his work life. That "something" turned out to be meaningful workplace friendships.

On paper, everything looked fine. He got along with his colleagues, delivered strong work, and kept things professional. But watching his teammates grab impromptu lunches together or collaborate on exciting projects, he felt like an outsider looking in. While others had formed natural alliances and friendships, Jordan found himself eating lunch alone, scrolling through his phone instead of sharing stories and ideas.

The path from colleague to friend isn't always obvious. Like many of us, Jordan had been socialized to believe that friendships should happen naturally—that putting conscious effort into building relationships somehow made them less authentic or valuable. This cultural messaging tells us that "real" friendships form spontaneously, making us hesitant to take proactive steps toward connection. It's a mindset that leaves many of us waiting for relationships that never materialize.

What to Do

Surprisingly, the same strategic thinking that makes you effective at work can help you build meaningful connections. Once Jordan let go of the belief that intentional friendship-building was somehow "wrong," he discovered a whole new approach to workplace relationships.

Armed with this insight, he took small but purposeful steps. He started by writing down whom he might want to connect with. Each week, he invited one person from the list for coffee. Yes, it felt awkward at first—like asking someone on a professional "friend date." But here's the fascinating thing about human psychology: Most people are far more open to connection than we assume. It's the likability gap—while we worry about being rejected, others are usually delighted to be asked.

Jordan didn't stop there. He joined a workplace safety committee, turning his passion into an opportunity for natural connection. He started arriving early to meetings, discovering that these quiet moments before the official start time were perfect for genuine conversations. He learned to practice "conversational cathexis"—picking up on subtle cues about what others wanted to discuss and following those threads with genuine curiosity.

The real breakthrough came when Jordan realized that meaningful connections require vulnerability. He began sharing more of himself—not oversharing, but offering glimpses into his life that

179

Putting Happiness into Action

invited others to also share. He started to talk about his life outside of work. He joined Slack channels that aligned with his interests, and began showing up at more company events.

Most importantly, he expanded his vision of workplace friendship beyond his immediate team. He sought out mentors who could guide both his professional growth and his networking journey. What started as a deliberate strategy evolved into genuine connections that made his workdays not just more productive, but more fulfilling.

Success Metrics

Once Jordan started interacting with colleagues more, conversations and connection naturally followed.

While some of those coffee chats weren't a match, a couple of them turned into weekly sessions where he and his new friend bonded over workplace challenges and the latest episode of their favorite show. He started to speak up more in meetings and have some lighthearted banter with the other early birds before getting started. He looked forward to his weekly safety committee meetings, where it felt like everyone there was working together toward a common goal.

After six months, Jordan felt a lot better about his job. He was having regular meaningful conversations and was better integrated into the team. His reputation at work had grown and he felt like it was helping his chances for advancement. He had recently started working with a mentor from another department and felt like he had someone in his corner. And he didn't worry about whom to have lunch with anymore.

Jordan's workplace transformed from a space he merely occupied to a community he helped create. His story shows that while workplace friendships might seem like they should "just happen," that's truly never the case.

Framework Fundamentals for Jordan

Jordan opened himself up to friendship with a few tried-and-true techniques (see Chapter 3):

- **Starting with familiar faces:** Rather than "find new people," he worked on changing his relationships with the people he saw regularly.

- **Becoming an opener:** He kickstarted connection by improving his active listening and asking people good questions about themselves.

- **Talking about more than work:** By sharing more of himself, he gave his coworkers more ways to connect with him—while also making himself more comfortable.

What all of the scenarios in this chapter have in common is that you have more control over them than you think you do. Often it just takes stepping back and following through on a plan to radically transform challenges that seemed insurmountable. Every one of the people described here became happier by learning the strategies we've talked about in these pages and turning them into daily habits that changed their situation for the better.

Chapter 9

Cultivating Team Happiness
A Leader's How-To Guide

Imagine your most stressful day at work. Your manager walks in and you can read the tension in his face. He snaps at a colleague during stand-up and sends a curt email about missed deadlines. By lunch, the whole team is on edge.

Now imagine this instead: That same manager acknowledges the pressure everyone's under, shares a laugh about his own morning mishap, and turns the deadline discussion into a collaborative problem-solving session. Two different approaches, two entirely different team experiences. Workers say that a manager's impact on teams outweighs all other workplace factors combined, including compensation and workload. Your leadership style isn't just one element of team happiness—it's the foundation everything else is built upon.

But here's what we rarely discuss: The pressures of leadership (the constant decisions, the weight of responsibility, the loneliness at the top) can challenge even the most optimistic among us.

This chapter offers a dual perspective. First, we'll explore six common leadership problems from my coaching practice that will show you how to create an environment where your team can flourish (names have been changed). Each strategy builds on the happiness framework we discussed in Chapters 3–7, giving you practical ways to weave happiness into the culture of your team.

Then we'll turn the lens inward. Because the truth is, your team's happiness and your own are inextricably linked. I'll share battle-tested practices for navigating the unique challenges of leadership while maintaining your own sense of joy and purpose. Think of it as putting on your own oxygen mask first—not out of selfishness, but because your happiness naturally spreads to those who look to you for guidance.

The Secret to Friendship at Work? It's You

When Emily first came to me for coaching, she was frustrated and felt like she was failing as a leader. As a product development lead, she had a capable team that delivered solid work, but something was missing. The energy wasn't there. Team meetings felt like waiting rooms—people would file in silently, stare at their phones, then retreat back to their desks the moment they were finished.

During our coaching sessions, we talked about the importance of workplace friendships and a light bulb went on—Emily had never paid much attention to the relationships on her team. She didn't think it was her role to facilitate friendships or get involved at all, which is understandable. But if we want to create a culture of happiness, we need to pay attention to the relationships on our teams.

When she started to look at the team through this lens, she saw a quiet team—there was almost no friendly chit-chat. When she brought the subject up at one-on-ones, she found that her team wasn't talking with each other about their work problems and people didn't really hang out together. They were operating in silos. It hit her that this might be a big problem.

Emily had never been a fan of traditional team-building approaches, so she decided to try some experiments. She knew the usual fixes wouldn't work—no one wants to go through forced bonding activities or awkward happy hours. Instead, she started paying attention to what her team members cared about outside of work.

She noticed that James, one of her senior developers, was always sharing beautiful landscape photos on Slack but he was constantly apologizing for his sad-looking desk plants. Emily asked James if he'd be willing to give Kristen some photography tips for her social media side project. In return, Kristen offered to help James rescue his struggling houseplants.

A month later, Emily overheard them debating the merits of different grow lights over coffee. James was showing Kristen his latest macro shots of her thriving succulent collection. Something as simple as connecting two people through their actual interests had created a genuine friendship.

This gave Emily an idea. Instead of pushing her team to be more social, she could create natural opportunities for connection. She started hosting monthly "fix-it" sessions where the team would tackle persistent workplace annoyances together. One group finally solved their nightmare document approval process. Another redesigned the overcrowded break room. The conversations that started with "This drives me crazy" often ended with people discovering shared interests and frustrations beyond work.

Emily also noticed that their traditional brainstorming sessions were always dominated by the same loud voices. She experimented with silent brainstorming—everyone writing ideas on whiteboards without speaking. Suddenly, her quieter team members were contributing more. The exercise created an unexpected side effect: People started drawing silly doodles alongside their ideas, leading to running jokes that only the team understood.

Her most successful experiment was accidental. After a particularly rough presentation where everything went wrong, Emily shared the story with her team, including her mortifying realization that she'd been on camera with spinach stuck in her teeth. Instead of the awkward silence she expected, her team started sharing their own embarrassing moments. These conversations evolved into monthly

Cultivating Team Happiness

"disaster story" lunches where people would share their recent fails, from work blunders to dating disasters.

A year later, Emily's team felt different. The pre-meeting silence had been replaced by actual conversations. People were collaborating across projects without being prompted. When facing challenges, team members actually reached out to each other for help instead of struggling alone.

This wasn't just about making work more pleasant. The stronger connections led to better work. Problems got solved faster because people weren't afraid to ask for help. Ideas improved because everyone felt comfortable pushing back and building on each other's thoughts. The team's output was noticeably stronger, earning recognition from senior management.

Emily's approach worked because she focused on creating natural opportunities for connection rather than forcing interaction. She paid attention to her team members' real interests and struggles. Most importantly, she made it clear through her own behavior that it was okay to be human at work—to have interests beyond your job description, to make mistakes, and to need help sometimes.

Now Emily faces a new challenge as her team grows: how to maintain these authentic connections while scaling, as people clamor to join her team. But the foundation she built shows that workplace friendships don't have to be manufactured; they just need the right conditions to develop naturally.

How to Disagree Without Showing Disrespect

I have a theory that minor misunderstandings can bring people closer together. I light up when someone in a meeting finally says what they really think. Whether it's a curse word or a passionate challenge to the status quo, these moments of friction reveal what people actually care about. The trick isn't avoiding conflict; it's making sure people attack the flaws in the logic, not the person presenting it. Most breakthroughs start with someone being bold enough to say, "This doesn't make sense," and everyone else being secure enough to actually listen. Just keep the knives aimed at the ideas, not each other. Leaders shape this environment by showing their own comfort with pushback—actively inviting disagreement rather than just tolerating it.

Disagreeing with others' ideas while confirming their personal competence leads to stronger bonds and more productive discussions. So make a habit of prefacing critiques with sincere acknowledgment of the person's capabilities and past contributions.

Building Trust from Scratch: How Real Leaders Build Unshakable Trust

Here's a hard truth: Not all leaders are willing to do what it takes to build psychological safety. It starts with owning your mistakes and talking about them—because if you don't, no one else will. But it's also about modeling the behaviors you want your team to practice. You need to show them how to handle failure. You want your team to care more about getting better than about protecting themselves.

Take Joshua, for example. He was eager to create a more open, trusting, and collaborative environment, but he wasn't sure where to start. Our coaching sessions focused on three key areas: modeling accountability, reshaping decision-making, and fostering a culture of learning. Through our conversations, he gained clarity on how his own behavior could set the tone for the entire team.

The Blame Stops Here

When Joshua inherited his company's product launch team, he noticed a pattern: Team members deflected blame, hoarded information, missed deadlines, lacked accountability, and worked in silos. During his first major meeting for a high-stakes launch, the COO pointed out a critical error in the pricing model. Instead of letting his team squirm under pressure from senior leadership, Joshua did something unexpected.

He owned the mistake completely.

During the meeting, he said, "This happened under my watch. I take full responsibility." People shot each other looks around the table—everyone knew that Joshua had only been in the job for a week. Afterward, he approached the team members who had to fix the error and offered his help. He did not blame anyone else, but focused on the solution.

In the post-launch review meeting a few weeks later, he started by saying, "Let me share three ways I could have supported this project better." He then asked his team what they needed from him next time that they didn't get on this project. The changes people suggested were relatively minor (people knew he wasn't to blame and were probably still a little afraid to give hard feedback), but Joshua made sure the suggestions were implemented immediately.

The Wisdom of "I Don't Know"

In our coaching sessions, we had spent a great deal of time talking about how to build a team with trust. What does that look like? How do you build it? We discussed how the highest-performing leaders repair trust by taking accountability and blending confidence with a healthy dose of humility.

To build trust in his team, Joshua decided to reshape his decision-making. Instead of issuing directives, he led with transparency:

"Here's what I know, here's what I don't know, and here's where I need your expertise." When people pretend they know something that they don't actually know, it's a sure way to break trust. By admitting his own knowledge gaps, he made it safe for others to do the same.

Team meetings became more dynamic, with people openly challenging strategies. People understood that their ideas would be taken seriously. When a new piece of data contradicted a plan, the team adjusted course—not with frustration, but with enthusiasm.

Joshua also spoke about past wrong decisions that he'd made on his previous team and the cost of those decisions. Suddenly it became okay to try and find the flaw in any approach and people were volunteering information that they might have kept to themselves in the past.

Permission to Be Imperfect

He didn't stop there. To reinforce a culture of growth, Joshua made his own learning visible. He openly worked on new technical skills and even asked junior team members for help. One day, he turned to Stephanie, a young data analyst, and said, "You're really good at data visualizations. Can you walk me through how you approach them?" That small act sent a powerful message—learning wasn't just encouraged; it was expected.

Six months in, the transformation was undeniable. Collaboration skyrocketed. The team moved faster, failed smarter, and missed fewer deadlines. Information was no longer hoarded; challenges were no longer hidden. Why? Because Joshua had redefined leadership. He showed that accountability flows up, not just down. He proved that admitting limitations makes a leader stronger, not weaker. And he made it clear that trust isn't built through perfection—it's built through honesty and follow-through.

This combination of accountability and confident humility is a superpower. Leaders of teams that have a strong culture of trust and psychological safety understand a fundamental truth: Trust isn't about always having the right answer; it's about being honest, adaptable, and consistently following through.

A leader's ability to repair trust is just as important as avoiding mistakes in the first place. When leaders embrace accountability and confident humility, they:

- Create psychological safety, making it easier for teams to voice concerns.

- Build credibility over time, even through difficulties.

- Manage crises more effectively, as people trust their judgment and honesty.

Psychological safety doesn't happen by accident. It starts at the top. And the best leaders—whether they're running a product team, a country, or a company—aren't the ones who have all the answers. They're the ones who create an environment where finding better answers is possible.

An Easier Way to Have Difficult Conversations

Know your destination before starting the journey. What exactly do you want to accomplish with this difficult conversation? Having this clarity is like having GPS for a tricky discussion. Without it, you risk wandering into emotional detours or getting lost in tangents. When you've defined success—whether it's changing a specific behavior, solving a problem together, or simply creating shared understanding—you'll know when you've arrived. This mental preparation gives you confidence and keeps the conversation on track when emotions run high.

Let's face it—delivering tough messages is nobody's idea of a good time. But with the right approach, these conversations can transform from awkward encounters into catalysts for real growth:

- **Clarify the stakes.** Show them why this matters—not just for the company, but for their own success. Help them connect the dots between their actions and the ripple effects that might be invisible to them.

- **Establish shared territory.** Before diving into what's wrong, acknowledge what's right. This creates a foundation of psychological safety that lets people actually hear feedback instead of immediately going into defense mode.

- **Focus with precision.** Tackle one clear issue rather than unleashing a barrage of complaints. Vague feedback just leaves people confused about what to fix, while specific concerns create clarity.

- **Verify understanding.** The words you carefully chose might land completely differently than you intended. Create space for questions and reflection to make sure you're both actually talking about the same issue.

- **Craft next steps together.** Once you both see the challenge clearly, collaborative planning creates buy-in and clarity. When the path forward emerges from genuine dialogue rather than top-down directives, people actually follow through.

Why Shining a Light on Progress Really Matters

Thomas led the kind of team that other managers envied. They were smart, efficient, and consistently exceeded their sales quotas month after month. Leadership trusted them completely. Other regions wanted to emulate their approach. And yet Thomas couldn't shake the feeling that something was off.

His team wasn't overwhelmed or struggling. They weren't missing targets. But they also weren't engaged. Meetings felt stiff. Collaboration was minimal. When a big project wrapped successfully, the response was muted—no real excitement, just a quiet nod and a move to the next task.

At first, Thomas told himself this was just the reality of working with high performers. They held themselves to high standards, so maybe they just didn't stop to celebrate. But when he started having more candid one-on-ones, the pattern became clear. His team wasn't complaining—but they weren't energized, either. One person summed it up perfectly: "We're doing great work, but it doesn't really feel like a win."

That's when Thomas came to me for coaching. "I know something is missing," he admitted, "but I don't know what. My team isn't unhappy, but they're not . . . invested."

And if he didn't fix that? He knew exactly what would happen. High performers don't stick around when they feel like cogs in a machine.

We worked together to break down what was really going on. Thomas realized that while his team excelled at closing deals, they lacked a sense of ownership. They were so focused on hitting targets that they rarely took risks, questioned their approach, or felt a personal stake in their client relationships. They weren't burned out—but they were disconnected.

As we went through each part of the happiness framework, a light bulb went on when we got to progress. Thomas realized that his team was so focused on the next task that they'd lost track of the big picture. Every win had just become a chore to check off before starting the next challenge. Every accomplishment felt the same.

His team had lost sight of what was really important—how their work mattered to the team, to themselves, and to the organization as a whole. Yes, people need to know that they're making progress, but they also need to know that their work is making a difference and that their contributions are valued. They, as individuals, need to be seen.

This idea shifted Thomas's approach. He started looking for ways to highlight not just what his team was accomplishing, but why it mattered.

First, he helped each team member connect their individual skills to the bigger picture. When someone gave their first presentation to the board, he didn't just acknowledge the achievement—he pointed out how their insights had directly shaped the company's strategy. When his client relations director handled a difficult client with ease, Thomas reminded her that this wasn't just a personal win—it helped strengthen a key partnership for the organization. Progress became more than hitting project milestones, but recognizing how each person's skills were growing *and what kind of impact they were making on the team and on the organization.*

He also introduced a Challenge Log, tracking tough problems the team had solved. But instead of just using it as a tool for problem-solving, he reframed it: "Look at the impact we've had. Look at how our work makes a difference." The team started seeing themselves not just as performers, but as a group that shaped the company's success.

At the team level, he started holding quarterly reflection meetings. Each person shared the biggest challenges they were currently facing, and then they reviewed the list from the previous quarter. Seeing how many of those once-daunting problems had been solved was powerful. But Thomas added another step: He tied those solutions back to real outcomes for the company. Instead of just saying,

"Look how far we've come," he made sure the team saw how their work mattered to customers, to leadership, and to each other.

The shift was noticeable. Team members started speaking up more in meetings, taking more ownership of their work, and backing each other up. People weren't just proud of their progress—they were proud of their impact. The work hadn't changed, but the way they saw it had. And that made all the difference.

How Enthusiasm Architects Can Unleash Your Team's Optimism

"My team just seems flat," Rachel told me during our coaching session. "I've tried recognition programs, clear goals, even bringing in lunch. Nothing seems to spark that energy we need."

Rachel's challenge was common among the leaders I coach. She had all the mechanics of good management in place, but something essential was missing: genuine enthusiasm. Enthusiasm isn't just a nice-to-have emotional state—it's the fundamental fuel that powers optimism, and ultimately, performance.

Rachel described how she carefully distributed work among her team members, priding herself on fairness. Everyone got an equal mix of interesting projects and necessary but tedious tasks. "It seems fair on paper," she said, "but in practice, everyone focuses on the assignments they don't want."

I asked her if she thought fairness was the right goal. Her team didn't have a problem with a lack of fairness; they had a lack of enthusiasm.

This perspective shift was uncomfortable for Rachel. "But some work just isn't exciting," she countered. "Someone has to do the boring stuff."

"Is all that 'boring stuff' equally boring to everyone?" I asked.

That question stopped her. After thinking about it for a moment, she mentioned how she actually enjoyed certain administrative tasks that others found tedious—she liked organizing project plans, for example, because she could listen to music and get into a flow state.

This was our breakthrough moment.

Conquering the Enthusiasm Deficit

In our next session, Rachel shared her discoveries after having conversations with each team member about what energized them:

- Paul actually *loved* writing documentation, because it helped him think more clearly about the systems he was working on.
- Priya, who barely said a word in most meetings, got fired up about doing data analysis.
- Lisa, the youngest member of the team, enjoyed client conversations because she learned something new every time.

Rachel realized that her own assumptions about what was "good" versus "boring" work had been projected onto her team. In reality, enthusiasm patterns were different for everyone.

Together, we developed an approach for Rachel to become what I call an "enthusiasm architect"—a leader who deliberately builds structures that foster and channel enthusiasm:

- **Uncover enthusiasm triggers.** Beyond just asking what people enjoy, Rachel learned to watch for signs of natural engagement—when someone leaned forward in meetings, when their pace of speech quickened, or when they voluntarily elaborated on a topic.
- **Assign work with enthusiasm mapping.** While still ensuring equitable workloads, Rachel began aligning assignments

with natural energy sources. The goal wasn't to eliminate all tedious work, but to ensure everyone had enough enthusiasm-generating work to fuel their optimism.

- **Create enthusiasm partnerships.** Rachel paired team members with complementary enthusiasm patterns. Paul, who enjoyed documentation, worked with James, who needed development in that area but brought technical depth.

- **Protect enthusiasm time.** Rachel blocked calendars for "deep work" sessions where people could focus on aspects of work that generated enthusiasm, creating natural reservoirs of optimism.

Enthusiasm Is a Catalyst for Optimism

After a few months of this new approach, Rachel reported that her team had made some remarkable changes. People's enthusiasm for what genuinely energizes them had begun to spill over into everything else.

She described how the team's perspective had shifted from task-focused to possibility-focused—the essence of optimism. Problems that once seemed insurmountable were now approached with creative energy. Team members who had been reluctant to voice ideas were now actively contributing solutions.

The key insight for Rachel was recognizing that enthusiasm is the precursor to optimism. Without enthusiasm—that genuine spark of engagement—optimism becomes forced positivity that quickly burns out. By becoming an enthusiasm architect, she had built the foundation for sustainable optimism that could weather challenges and fuel innovation. She now saw herself as responsible for cultivating her team's energy as a resource, not just making sure the work gets done.

"The most powerful question I now ask isn't 'Who should do this work?'" Rachel said. "It's 'Who would bring enthusiasm to this work?' That single shift has transformed how my team functions and how they feel about their jobs."

For leaders facing disengagement, this approach offers a practical path forward: Build enthusiasm first, and optimism will naturally follow.

Leaders Who Use Enthusiasm to Inspire

The best leaders understand the power of enthusiasm to inspire their team. Their energy and positivity signals that they have confidence in the team's direction and the possibilities that lie ahead. These leaders offer a great example:

- Richard Branson's always-upbeat attitude tells his employees that he trusts them and he's not afraid to take risks.

- Oprah Winfrey uses her excitement about empowering others to get people to join her.

- Howard Schultz built Starbucks by enthusiastically promoting coffee as a way to build community.

Who will be your role model? Think about leaders you admire who use enthusiasm as a tool and see if you can bring that same energy to your team.

Give Your Team Maximum Autonomy (Even If It Makes You Nervous)

"I'm not micromanaging, am I?" Nadia asked during our coaching session, her voice tense. "I give my team space, but sometimes they head in directions that just won't work."

This wasn't an unusual concern. As I've coached dozens of first-time managers, I've repeatedly seen this pattern: capable professionals, who've built their careers on taking action, suddenly struggling with doing less.

When I first started working with Nadia, she proudly described her hands-off approach. "I don't hover. I let them run with projects." But as our sessions continued, a different picture emerged.

"I had to jump in yesterday," she said in our third meeting. "They were about to present a strategy to the VP that missed a critical market factor. I just gave them a few tweaks."

When I asked how often she made these small adjustments, she paused, then laughed. "At least twice a week. But they're always quick—just sharing my experience."

What Nadia was actually practicing wasn't autonomy but unpredictable intervention—arguably worse than consistent micromanagement. Her team never knew when she might suddenly appear with "suggestions" that felt like mandates.

I asked Nadia to watch her team's body language when they presented ideas to her. "They're tense," she admitted. "They rush through presentations like they're waiting for me to cut in."

We discussed how her "helpful tweaks" were actually sending a powerful message: that she didn't trust their judgment.

Nadia admitted that she struggled with this. She wanted her team to benefit from her 15 years of experience and she wanted to add value.

"There's a difference between offering experience and hijacking decisions," I explained. "One builds capability; the other creates dependency."

Define the Edges, Not the Path

Together, we developed a new approach that I've seen transform dozens of leadership relationships. Instead of giving freedom with invisible strings attached, Nadia would clearly define:

- **Nonnegotiable constraints.** These are genuine business requirements: "We have a $50K budget, a six-week timeline, and we can't change our pricing structure."

- **Measurable objectives.** Rather than prescribing solutions, Nadia would focus on outcomes: "We need to reduce customer service calls by 30 percent while maintaining satisfaction ratings."

- **Escalation triggers.** Instead of requiring constant check-ins, she identified specific conditions that warranted her involvement: "Come to me if the projected timeline extends beyond eight weeks or if customer satisfaction drops more than 10 percent."

The most challenging part of our work together came when I suggested a radical step: telling Nadia's team they could no longer ask for her approval.

"They can't just do whatever they want," she protested. "I'm accountable for their work."

"That's not what I'm suggesting," I clarified. "They must make a clear decision and explain their reasoning to you. You can challenge their thinking, but they're responsible for the choice."

Nadia was hesitant, but agreed to try it. It wasn't long before someone came to her and asked, "What do you think we should do?" She knew this was the critical moment where the whole strategy would fall apart if she gave the wrong answer. She smiled and just said, "I think you should make a clear choice and help me understand why it's right."

Her team member looked startled, then thoughtful. Two days later, she returned with a detailed proposal that addressed issues Nadia hadn't even considered.

The Transformation

In our follow-up sessions, Nadia reported a striking change. Her initial anxiety ("Are they going to crash and burn?") gradually transformed into curiosity ("I wonder what approach they'll take?") and finally into confidence ("They consistently see angles that I don't.").

The most unexpected outcome? Her team began setting higher standards than she would have. This pattern repeated across projects: Given genuine autonomy, her team became more rigorous, not less. They stopped looking for safe answers and started finding innovative ones.

The payoff extended beyond better decisions. Meetings that once felt like approval sessions became genuine strategy discussions.

Nadia had come to understand the power of trust. By giving her team genuine autonomy, she'd shown them that she trusted their judgment. Her team had responded by trusting her more, knowing that their risks would be rewarded.

This is a core principle of my framework for team happiness: Trust functions as both foundation and outcome. When leaders demonstrate trust by granting meaningful autonomy, it creates a virtuous cycle that elevates team performance and satisfaction.

"I used to think my value came from having the right answers," Nadia said. "Now I realize it comes from creating the right conditions. My anxiety about letting go was really about my ego, not their capability."

Trust Has a Multiplier Effect

Trust acts as a multiplier for the other elements of team happiness. When team members operate in a high-trust environment with meaningful autonomy:

- Their **connection** deepens as they collaborate without fear of judgment.
- Their **resilience** strengthens because they feel empowered to solve problems.

- Their sense of **progress** amplifies when they own both the path and the outcome.

- Their **optimism** grows from confidence in their collective capabilities.

"The strangest part," Nadia told me in our final session, "is that I feel more influential now that I exercise less direct control. By doing less, I've accomplished more."

For any leader struggling with the balance between guidance and control, remember: True autonomy isn't about abandoning your team to figure things out alone. It's about clearly defining the boundaries, then trusting them to find the best path.

Your team can handle more responsibility than you think. The question is whether you can handle giving it to them—and in doing so, create the foundation of trust that makes sustainable team happiness possible.

Transform Learning into Results: How Smart Leaders Turn Development into Dollars

"Let me get this straight," the VP said, leaning back in his chair. "You want to send your stockroom guy to a supply chain management course?"

Rita nodded confidently. "Marco's reorganization of our inventory system cut processing time by 25 percent last quarter—with no formal training. Imagine what he could do with actual skills."

The VP studied the proposal in front of him. "And you're projecting another 15 percent efficiency gain?"

"Conservative estimate," Rita replied. "I've included three comparable case studies."

This wasn't the first time Rita had made such a request, nor would it be the last. But her approach had fundamentally changed how her company viewed employee development.

The Learning-Results Connection

Rita's journey began when she noticed a pattern in her own career: Her biggest contributions always came after learning something new. Yet in leadership meetings, training budgets were treated like corporate luxury items—nice to have in good times, first to be cut in lean ones.

"We're thinking about this backward," she told me. "Learning isn't a reward for good performance—it's the engine that drives it."

But Rita knew that philosophical arguments wouldn't sway her metrics-focused executives. She needed data.

Instead of starting with training opportunities, we decided that Rita should begin with untapped talent. She developed three questions that revealed where her team members' natural energy and aptitude lay:

- What problems do you find yourself solving even when no one asks you to?
- When do colleagues specifically seek you out for help?
- What aspects of your work leave you with more energy than when you started?

The responses revealed goldmines of potential. Ian, a five-year veteran, lit up when mentoring new hires. Melody's merchandising experiments in her section had quietly outperformed the rest of the store. Keisha, despite being in the same role for years, obsessed over streamlining seasonal display setups.

These weren't just preferences. These questions revealed undeveloped talent veins running through her team.

From Learning to Earning

Rita's breakthrough came when she stopped selling learning to her executive team and started selling outcomes. Each proposal followed the same formula:

- **Evidence of untapped potential:** "Marco's stockroom reorganization saved us 120 labor hours last quarter."

- **Targeted learning investment:** "This supply chain certification costs $2,200 and requires 40 hours of his time."

- **Projected business impact:** "Based on similar implementations, we project annual savings of $37,000 and 15 percent faster inventory turns."

The results were immediate. Not only were her requests approved, but her team's development budget doubled within a year—because each investment delivered measurable returns.

The real magic happened when Rita's team caught on. Instead of waiting for development opportunities, they began identifying business problems that aligned with their interests.

Keisha approached Rita with spreadsheets in hand. "Our seasonal display changeovers eat up 180 labor hours quarterly. If I learn better project management methods, I can cut that by 30 percent."

"The cost?" Rita asked.

"$1,800 for the certification. Pays for itself in one season."

Rita smiled. "Draft the proposal. I'll take it upstairs tomorrow."

As word spread, team members began seeing business challenges differently. Problems weren't just obstacles to overcome—they were opportunities to grow. A customer service bottleneck became Jamal's chance to learn process improvement methodologies. Recurring inventory discrepancies became Lin's opportunity to master data analysis.

The Hidden ROI

The financial returns were easily measured: efficiency gains, sales increases, error reductions. But Rita tracked subtler metrics, too. Team turnover dropped from 22 percent to 8 percent annually. Internal promotions tripled. Employee engagement scores rose from the bottom quartile to the top 15 percent.

"The traditional approach treats learning as a cost," Rita explained to her skeptical colleagues. "But when it's driven by business needs and measured by outcomes, it becomes your highest-ROI investment."

Most compelling was what happened when budget cuts loomed. The CFO wanted across-the-board reductions. Instead of accepting her share, Rita presented the three-year ROI data from her team's development investments: a 341 percent return.

Her department's learning budget was the only one spared from cuts.

Learning Is the Engine of Progress

What Rita discovered connects directly to one of the most powerful parts of my framework for team happiness: progress. Through our coaching sessions, she came to understand that meaningful progress—both personal and professional—is not just about moving metrics. It's about growing capabilities that make improving those metrics possible.

"I used to think progress just meant hitting targets faster," Rita told me in our final coaching session. "Now I see it's about expanding what's possible in the first place."

This insight transformed how her team experienced work. Through learning opportunities tied to business outcomes, team members weren't just completing tasks—they were becoming visibly more capable. This created a powerful dual sense of progress: advancing business goals while simultaneously advancing personal development.

Research consistently shows that people's most satisfying days at work are those where they make tangible progress. Rita's approach supercharged this effect by making progress multidimensional:

- **Skill progress:** "I can do things today I couldn't do six months ago."

- **Career progress:** "I'm building capabilities that increase my value."

- **Impact progress:** "My contributions create measurable improvements."

- **Team progress:** "We're collectively solving bigger problems than before."

Her approach created a culture where learning and performance became inseparable partners in a virtuous cycle. People developed skills that improved results, which justified more development, which improved more results—a continuous upward spiral of progress.

By reframing learning as an investment with measurable returns, Rita transformed how her organization viewed human potential—not as a fixed asset to deploy, but as an appreciating investment that grows in value with each added capability.

For leaders seeking both better results and more engaged teams, recognize that learning creates the profound sense of progress that lies at the heart of workplace happiness. Don't treat learning as a perk. Treat it as your most powerful engine for meaningful progress that energizes both individuals and organizations.

Know Your Own Happiness Obstacles

Here's the brutal truth: Being happy at work is harder for managers and leaders than it is for regular employees. Leadership comes with its own unique stresses and challenges.

For starters, it's lonely at the top. Over time, this loneliness takes a toll on both your work performance and your well-being. Work puts up all sorts of obstacles to developing close connections with others:

- **Power dynamics:** Most interactions that leaders have revolve around using their authority, rather than having a collaboration that leads to genuine connection. Their authority creates distance between them and the people they lead. Leadership roles often require difficult decisions that can alienate others.

- **Relationship barriers:** The need to maintain professional boundaries makes authentic connections more difficult and prevents deeper relationships from forming. Those relationships are more complicated because leaders don't always know if someone is responding to them or their position.

- **Maintaining an image:** Leaders are expected to maintain a strong, capable image and handle negative emotions privately. They worry that showing vulnerability could be perceived as weakness.

- **Heightened pressure:** Leaders often feel pressured to be "on" at all times and manage others' emotions while suppressing their own. Work demands leave little time to invest in relationship building.

- **Lack of peer support:** Leaders have few opportunities to connect with peers who understand their unique challenges.

Workplace friendships are more difficult at higher levels, especially when colleagues may be competing with you for prestige positions.

For these reasons, loneliness can be harder to overcome through the relationship-building strategies that people used earlier in their careers. Because relationships don't form "naturally" as easily as before, leaders need to put more time into nurturing deep relationships than they have in the past.

All of this means that leaders need to work harder than anyone to build meaningful relationships.

Many leaders choose to ignore the problem—there's always a fire to put out that you can use as an excuse—but your team needs you to be happy. It's hard to ask people to be optimistic and resilient if you're frustrated and fragile. You can't inspire others if you don't have your own house in order. So leaders need to pay attention to their own happiness—so they can help others find theirs.

Everyone should pursue their own happiness needs, but leaders should keep these things in mind:

- **Pay attention to your personal relationships.** Is all your social time consumed with work responsibilities? Friendships outside of work are crucial for mental well-being. Time with friends and family should be nonnegotiable (and there's nothing wrong with adding it to your calendar).

- **Pursue your hobbies.** Making time for your passions is the best way to turn off your work brain and really recharge.

- **Don't make burnout a badge of honor.** Everyone says they're really busy, but few have the courage to add "Actually, I'm feeling pretty burned out." Being vulnerable is the first step to honest conversations and addressing the problem shows your team that they should also look after themselves.

Balance means something different for everyone. Investing in your passions and relationships outside of work can make it easier to bring the best version of yourself to the office. To help others, you sometimes need to help yourself.

Chapter 10

Yes, You Can Actually Love Your Work
The Surprising Path to Workplace Happiness

When I tell people about this deli in Michigan where new employees learn to read financial statements their first week, and where everyone—from dishwashers to managers—has a voice in major business decisions, I watch their expressions shift from fascination to doubt. "Nice story," they say, "but that can't work in a real company like mine." I hear the unspoken question: Are these workplace happiness practices just fantasy for those of us trapped in traditional jobs?

After studying thriving organizations across industries and continents, I can tell you this: Happiness at work isn't some far-fetched dream. It's happening right now in places you'd never expect.

That place is Zingerman's Deli in Ann Arbor, Michigan. Every time I visit, the line stretches out the door, winding past their window displays of artisanal olive oils, aged vinegars, and freshly baked breads. The aroma is intoxicating—a mix of fresh-baked rye, house-cured corned beef, and that coffee cake that haunts my dreams.

Inside, it's organized chaos in the best possible way. Customers point at the chalkboard menu that covers an entire wall, debating between the Binny's Brooklyn Reuben (hand-sliced pastrami, Swiss cheese, sauerkraut on grilled pumpernickel) or the #2 Zingerman's

Reuben (with locally made Russian dressing that makes you question everything you thought you knew about sandwiches).

Behind the counter, there's this incredible dance happening. Staff calling out orders, slicing meats paper-thin, building these monumental sandwiches that make your regular deli look like amateur hour. But what caught my attention on my last visit wasn't just the food—it was a conversation I overheard while waiting in line.

I met Melissa, who was in her first week on the job. Now, you'd expect her to be learning how to build these masterpiece sandwiches or memorizing their extensive menu. Instead, she's sitting in the back room, learning to read financial statements. Yes, you read that right. At Zingerman's, everyone—from the person slicing your corned beef to the person making your latkes—learns the business numbers.

During her first week, Melissa sits in on a huddle where the team is discussing a challenge: Cheese costs have risen 20 percent. In most businesses, this would be a closed-door management discussion, probably involving a lot of stern faces and spreadsheets. But at Zingerman's the entire team brainstorms solutions. A line cook who's been experimenting with different cheese suppliers suggests a new vendor. A server who notices customer ordering patterns proposes adjusting portion sizes on certain dishes. And Melissa, despite being almost newer than the bread they baked that morning, shares an idea about special promotions.

Three months later, I came back (the coffee cake called to me, what can I say?) and Melissa's story had taken an amazing turn. She'd joined a "mini-business" within Zingerman's—a catering company that was spun out after staff noticed how many customers asked about private events. She has access to all the numbers, makes real decisions, and is able to follow her passion within the company.

This is what makes Zingerman's different from our earlier Four Seasons story in Chapter 5. While the Four Seasons made it okay to talk about mistakes, Zingerman's takes psychological safety to a whole new level—they encourage staff to understand and influence the entire business. They've created an environment where a new hire feels comfortable suggesting solutions to rising cheese costs, where a line cook can influence supplier decisions, and where everyone understands how their role contributes to success.

As Ari Weinzweig, Zingerman's co-founder, says, "When you give people responsibility without information, you create helplessness. When you give them information without responsibility, you create cynicism. But when you give both, you create engagement."[1]

The results? Forty years of growth. Industry-leading employee retention. And yes, the best sandwiches in America. But more importantly, they've created a place where trust isn't just talked about—it's baked into every decision, every day, just like that incredible coffee cake I can't stop thinking about.

Zingerman's Secret Ingredient

What I love about Zingerman's isn't just that they're naturally following each step of my happiness framework—they're bringing it to life in ways that transform everyone who walks through their doors. Their optimism and enthusiasm infuse everything from Ari Weinzweig's visionary leadership philosophy to the way staff eagerly share their passion for artisanal foods with wide-eyed customers. Progress isn't just a business metric there—it's woven into forty years of continuous innovation, where growth comes not from scaling up but from nurturing new ideas from within. The trust and psychological safety are so tangible that new employees like Melissa find themselves confidently sharing financial insights during their first week. Resilience flourishes through their University

(continued)

Yes, You Can Actually Love Your Work

(continued)

of Zingerman's, where setbacks become learning opportunities and every challenge sparks creative problem-solving. And perhaps most visibly, connection and friendship radiate through the deliberate chaos behind the counter—a choreographed dance of collaboration where laughter punctuates the serious business of creating the perfect sandwich. At Zingerman's, happiness isn't an abstract concept—it's their secret ingredient.

Zingerman's approach has captured the attention of business leaders, consumers, and media alike, earning them widespread recognition and accolades. *Harvard Business Review*, among the most respected voices in management thinking, found their model so compelling that they published an in-depth case study exploring the inner workings of this culinary phenomenon. The analysis revealed how Zingerman's distinctive practices around trust and psychological safety have created not just a successful business, but a transformative workplace culture that delights both employees and customers, challenging conventional wisdom about organizational design and how consumer loyalty is built through authentic engagement:

> Imagine walking into a business where every employee acts like an owner. That's what caught *Harvard Business Review*'s attention about Zingerman's. They created something called the Community of Businesses: a network of independent but interconnected companies, each partner-owned, all sharing the same values. But what's fascinating is how they build trust into this structure.
>
> Take their "Path to Empowerment" program. It's not just about learning to make great sandwiches. Every employee,

regardless of position, learns the business inside and out. They study financial statements, understand business metrics, and learn leadership skills. It's like getting a mini-MBA while working at a deli.

But here's where psychological safety really shows up: In their weekly huddles, staff don't just review numbers—they debate them. Question them. Suggest improvements. A delivery driver might challenge a financial projection. A line cook might propose a new business venture. And they're not just heard—they're taken seriously.[2]

This connects directly to what we saw at the Four Seasons. While the Glitch Report made it safe to discuss mistakes, Zingerman's makes it safe to question everything, from how they make sandwiches to how they make decisions. They've created an environment where every voice matters, where entrepreneurial thinking isn't just encouraged; it's expected.

The result? They've grown from a single deli to a community of sixteen businesses, each started by former employees who came up through this system. Trust isn't just a concept—it's the secret ingredient in everything they do.

As one employee beautifully put it, "There was no ceiling. Later on, I moved to accounting. Open-book finance had a lot to do with it."[3]

Zingerman's shows us what happens when you build a business around happiness. Their open-book approach creates the trust that makes people feel safe to speak up and share ideas. Their dedication to teaching everyone—from sandwich makers to managers—helps build resilience through continuous learning. And most importantly, they truly believe in what each person can bring to the table, no matter their position or experience. The result? Not just great sandwiches and business success, but a place where people genuinely connect, grow, and look forward to coming to work each day. At Zingerman's, we see how trust, learning, and believing in people creates a workplace where happiness isn't just a nice bonus—it's the engine that powers everything they do.

A Different Kind of "Lunch and Learn"

Learning is such a core value at Zingerman's that they don't stop at offering a training program—employees are part of a comprehensive learning system called University of Zingerman's. Every employee can:

- Earn University of Zingerman's degrees within the company.
- Receive cash rewards for completing educational milestones.
- Attend courses ranging from food knowledge to financial management.
- Receive scholarships to pursue learning opportunities outside the company.

This dedication to ongoing learning doesn't just build knowledge—it cultivates the inner strength employees need to navigate challenges confidently while fostering an atmosphere where possibility and optimism flourish naturally in everyday interactions.

Visions of Workplace Happiness from Around the World

While Zingerman's stands out as a remarkable place to work, it's easy to see it as an exception—a rare success story amid the grinding reality of typical jobs. You might think, "Sure, that works for a quirky deli in Ann Arbor, Michigan, but what about the rest of us?" It's tempting to write off these happiness practices as a dream world for those trapped in corporate hierarchies, or to believe they're only possible with extraordinary leadership.

I challenge that assumption—it's simply not true. The stories and research throughout this book predominantly come from American soil, yet if we venture beyond our borders, we discover fascinating and completely achievable examples of practices that create genuine happiness, satisfaction, and fulfillment throughout entire organizations. All of the traditions in the following sections lead to things that are often sorely lacking in fast-paced American workplaces: lower stress levels, stronger team bonds, and greater job satisfaction. By baking these happiness habits into their workplace culture, workers in these countries are highly productive without the burnout that is familiar to so many of us.

Sweden: Making Time for Conversation and Connection

Take Sweden (home of Spotify), for example. For decades, *fika* (coffee breaks) have been a cultural institution and a central part of Swedish life. Like Zingerman's, mouthwatering baked goods play an important role, but the secret here is ritualized connection. People stop what they're doing, often several times a day, to savor a cup of coffee and enjoy something sweet with friends, family, or work colleagues.

Most workplaces have dedicated *fika* rooms and schedule two 15–30 minute breaks daily (at around 10 a.m. and 3 p.m.). During *fika*, work discussion is generally avoided in favor of personal connection. Many people bake treats at home (there's an element of friendly competition) and bring them in, but companies also provide pastries and snacks. It's such an ingrained part of Swedish life that it's considered impolite to skip *fika* or take it at your desk.

During these leisurely breaks, coworkers and management mingle easily and the conversations range widely. It's normal for people to express their views, and because everyone takes the break together, people feel like their voices are heard. As you can imagine, this regular socializing makes it a lot easier for people to form friendships beyond their team or their rung on the corporate ladder. And time to recharge is automatically built into everyone's schedule.

You might be wondering: Don't all these coffee breaks slow down work? The short answer is: no. Sweden is ranked a very respectable 11th in the world for GDP per hour of work.[4] People come back from these breaks energized and focused (and not just from the caffeine).

Japan: An Early Start on Happiness Habits

Japan also offers us some fascinating lessons—and they start well before people reach working age.

Step into a Japanese primary school, and you'll witness something magical happening. Seven-year-olds grab brooms and mops with enthusiasm, cleaning their classrooms together while chatting and laughing. At lunchtime, these same kids—wearing adorable aprons and face masks—proudly serve steaming rice and miso soup to their friends. Each morning, a different child stands confidently at the front of the room, leading classmates through announcements and assigning the day's tasks. Some kids bounce with excitement when it's their turn to organize sports equipment, others beam with pride when planning classroom celebrations, and the animal lovers practically glow when feeding the classroom hamster or tending to plants. All the while, their teacher simply watches from the sidelines, offering a gentle suggestion here and there—more coach than boss.[5]

This scene might seem like an impossible fantasy in American education, but in Japan, it's simply Tuesday. These children aren't just completing chores—they're building the essential happiness habits that will serve them for life: resilience when faced with challenges, mastery of practical skills, the thrill of genuine autonomy, and unwavering trust in their community. These are the exact same ingredients that create thriving, innovative teams in the workplace.

As these students grow, their collaborative spirit intensifies. By sixth grade, classmates transform into architectural engineers of human pyramids called *kumitaiso*—towering structures of interlinked bodies requiring perfect balance and communication.[6] During weeks of practice, they tumble and fall, laugh and try again, each attempt strengthening their resilience muscles and delivering that intoxicating rush of improvement that comes only through shared struggle and triumph.

Imagine if your team approached challenges with this same mindset—where setbacks become steppingstones, where every team member understands their crucial role in supporting others, and where collective achievement generates the kind of authentic happiness that no office perks could ever match. This isn't just education; it's a blueprint for building teams where people flourish together.

The Netherlands: How Equality Builds Trust

All of this can seem remarkable to people from an individualistic culture like that of the United States. That's what makes it so interesting to look at places with different viewpoints and see how it affects how they work. In the Netherlands, for example, people are famous for being egalitarian and very focused on fairness.

This shows up in the very structure of Dutch workplaces. Most office layouts feature open "social corners" with coffee machines and seating for people to connect. Managers are expected to be approachable and remote workers are actively included in team activities. On your birthday, everyone in the office gets together to celebrate, but it's the responsibility of the person having the birthday to bring the treats (and you better bring enough for everyone).

This strong emphasis on fairness keeps trust in your colleagues high, which makes it easier to build strong social bonds. People don't work through lunch, but look at it as an opportunity for connection. The Netherlands also has a tradition called *borrelen*—which means gathering with your coworkers for *borrel* (usually drinks and some delicious deep-fried snacks) at the end of the work week. These informal gatherings—which can happen in the office or at a local watering hole—are a celebration of the week's progress and a chance for intergenerational mingling, before people split up to meet friends and family for dinner.[7]

Happiness as Strategy: The Science of Thriving at Work

Once in a while, at one of my workshops, someone raises their hand and asks, "Why do we need to be happy at work? Isn't work just meant to fund our actual lives?" The question is often accompanied by knowing glances around the room.

The truth is simpler than most people realize: Our brains don't recognize the artificial boundary between work and home. The emotions you experience at 3 p.m. don't magically reset when you walk through your front door at 6 p.m. That frustration from a difficult meeting travels with you. But so does the satisfaction of solving a challenging problem or the warmth of a genuine connection with a colleague.

What's remarkable is how this ripple effect transforms organizations. Teams that are flourishing and fulfilled and happy at work consistently outperform their competitors—they're more creative, more productive, and substantially more likely to stay. When people feel genuinely good about their work environment, they bring their best thinking, their most innovative ideas, and their authentic selves to the table.

I've witnessed this transformation countless times. A manufacturing team in Detroit implemented simple daily appreciation practices and saw quality metrics improve by double digits within months. A technology startup in Austin created structured time for meaningful connection, and their turnover dropped dramatically while customer satisfaction scores soared.

Remember Maria from the book's introduction? She was able to overcome her seemingly insurmountable problems by putting the happiness framework to work:

- She replaced the hole created when her best friend left by consciously seeking out connection with her colleagues. Using the power of the "mere exposure effect" and the "likability gap," she soon had more (and better) relationships than she ever had before.

- She built up her resilience by focusing on growing her own mastery (and looking for someone to help when she was feeling down).

- She grew her team's trust in each other by modeling transparency and vulnerability, including creating her own version of the Glitch Report.

- She designed her day to make progress and momentum inevitable.

- She embraced an upbeat enthusiasm that proved to be contagious and ended up drawing people to her.

These outcomes aren't accidents or anomalies. The science is clear that our brains work better in positive emotional states. We literally see more possibilities (our peripheral vision literally increases!), make better decisions, and collaborate more effectively when we're experiencing positive emotions at work.[8]

Here's what's most empowering: Happiness at work isn't determined primarily by your title, your salary, or even your company culture. While those external factors matter, they account for less than a quarter of workplace well-being. The rest comes from internal frameworks and habits that you can intentionally develop.

This isn't about pretending everything is perfect or plastering on a fake smile. It's about implementing specific, evidence-based approaches that transform work from something we endure into something that enhances our lives. It's about creating an environment where Sunday evening brings on anticipation rather than dread, where your energy expands rather than depletes as the week progresses.

You might not be experiencing this reality right now. Your workplace might seem miles away from what I'm describing. But I've guided thousands of people through this journey, and I can tell you with absolute certainty that this transformation is possible for you.

The path forward is clear: Build meaningful workplace relationships; develop resilience through deliberate practice; establish environments of trust through small, consistent actions; create systems that enable regular progress; and cultivate realistic optimism through how you interpret events.

Start small. Choose one area that resonates most strongly and take a single action tomorrow. The data is clear that consistent microhabits create more lasting change than dramatic overhauls. Your capacity for workplace happiness follows the same principles as any other skill—it develops through informed, persistent effort.

The evidence speaks for itself: You can transform your experience of work. And when you do, that transformation will ripple through every other aspect of your life.

Notes

Chapter 1

1. "Capitalism Can't Give Us Meaningful Work," October 24, 2020. https://jacobin.com/2020/10/capitalism-work-hours-worked-over-american-dream.

2. Shawn Achor, Andrew Reece, Gabriella Rosen Kellerman, and Alexi Robichaux. "9 Out of 10 People Are Willing to Earn Less Money to Do More-Meaningful Work." *Harvard Business Review*, November 6, 2018. https://hbr.org/2018/11/9-out-of-10-people-are-willing-to-earn-less-money-to-do-more-meaningful-work.

3. Kate Morgan. "The Great Resignation Is 'Over,'" August 2, 2023. https://www.bbc.com/worklife/article/20230731-the-great-resignation-is-over-what-does-that-mean.

4. Suzanne Blake. "Thousands of Americans Quit Their Jobs." *Newsweek*, May 8, 2024. https://www.newsweek.com/thousands-americans-quit-their-jobs-1898528.

5. SuperStaff. "Employee Engagement Plummets to Record Low, Gallup Reports." *Philippine Outsourcing & BPO Call Center Services | SuperStaff* (blog), August 21, 2024. https://www.superstaff.com/blog/employee-engagement-plummets/#:~:text=The%20assumption%20is%20true%3A%20Engaged,more%20motivated%20to%20work%20hard.

6. Shawn Achor. "Positive Intelligence." *Harvard Business Review*, January 1, 2012. https://hbr.org/2012/01/positive-intelligence.

7. Ted Kitterman. "When Employees Thrive, Companies More Than Triple Their Stock Market Performance." Great Place to Work®, n.d. https://www.greatplacetowork.com/resources/blog/when-employees-thrive-companies-triple-their-stock-market-performance.

8. Daniel Kahneman and Angus Deaton. "High Income Improves Evaluation of Life but Not Emotional Well-being." *Proceedings of the National Academy of Sciences* 107, no. 38 (September 7, 2010): 16489–93. https://doi.org/10.1073/pnas.1011492107.

9. David Greene and Mark R. Lepper. "Effects of Extrinsic Rewards on Children's Subsequent Intrinsic Interest." *Child Development* 45, no. 4 (1974): 1141–45. https://doi.org/10.2307/1128110.

10. Kathy Gurchiek. "Survey: Respect at Work Boosts Job Satisfaction." *SHRM*, December 21, 2023. https://www.shrm.org/topics-tools/news/employee-relations/survey-respect-work-boosts-job-satisfaction?utm_source.

11. Nicole Celestine. "Broaden-and-Build Theory of Positive Emotions." *Positive Psychology,* August 30, 2016. Accessed March 18, 2025. https://positivepsychology.com/broaden-build-theory/.

12. Karl A. Phillips, Naykky Singh Ospina, and Victor M. Montori. "Physicians Interrupting Patients." *Journal of General Internal Medicine* 34, no. 10 (August 6, 2019): 1965. https://doi.org/10.1007/s11606-019-05247-5.

13. Tanya Lewis. "Twins Separated at Birth Reveal Staggering Influence of Genetics." Livescience, August 11, 2014. https://www.livescience.com/47288-twin-study-importance-of-genetics.html/.

14. Liz Mineo. "Good Genes Are Nice, but Joy Is Better." *Harvard Gazette*, January 11, 2024. https://news.harvard.edu/gazette/story/2017/04/over-nearly-80-years-harvard-study-has-been-showing-how-to-live-a-healthy-and-happy-life/.

15. Melissa Madeson. "Seligman's PERMA+ Model Explained: A Theory of Wellbeing." *Positive Psychology,* February 24, 2017. Accessed March 18, 2025. https://positivepsychology.com/perma-model/.

Chapter 2

1. "Blue Zones Institute: Research Evidence." Blue Zones, October 24, 2024. https://www.bluezones.com/blue-zones-institute-research-evidence/.

2. Dan Buettner. *The Blue Zones of Happiness: Lessons from the World's Happiest People.* National Geographic Books, 2017.

3. Denmark.dk. "What Do We Mean by "Hygge?," n.d. https://denmark.dk/people-and-culture/hygge.

4. Wikipedia contributors. "List of Countries by Labour Productivity." Wikipedia, February 11, 2025. https://en.wikipedia.org/wiki/List_of_countries_by_labour_productivity.

5. Robert Waldinger. "What Makes a Good Life? Lessons from the Longest Study on Happiness," November 2015. Accessed March 18, 2025. https://www.ted.com/talks/robert_waldinger_what_makes_a_good_life_lessons_from_the_longest_study_on_happiness.

6. Neuroscience News. "Social Bonds Protect Aging Brains." *Neuroscience News*, June 20, 2023. https://neurosciencenews.com/social-aging-neuroscience-brain-23505/.

7. Kosuke Sato and Masaki Yuki, "The Association Between Self-esteem and Happiness Differs in Relationally Mobile vs. Stable Interpersonal Contexts." *Frontiers in Psychology* 5 (October 9, 2014). https://doi.org/10.3389/fpsyg.2014.01113.

8. Arash Emamzadeh. "The Essential Ingredient for Happiness and Well-Being . . . And What to Do if You Feel You're Missing It." *Psychology Today*, January 19, 2022. https://www.psychologytoday.com/ca/blog/finding-new-home/202201/the-essential-ingredient-happiness-and-well-being.

9. Timothy A. Pychyl. "How to Decrease Procrastination and Increase Happiness." *Psychology Today*, June 7, 2008. https://www.psychologytoday.com/ca/blog/dont-delay/200806/goal-progress-and-happiness.

10. Tracy Brower. "Learning Is a Sure Path to Happiness: Science Proves It." *Forbes,* October 17, 2021. https://www.forbes.com/sites/tracybrower/2021/10/17/learning-is-a-sure-path-to-happiness-science-proves-it/.

11. "APA PsycNet," n.d. https://psycnet.apa.org/record/2001-16970-007.

12. J.D. Kammeyer-Mueller, T.A. Judge, and B.A. Livingston. (2008). "Psychological Ownership and Organizational Citizenship Behavior." *Journal of Applied Psychology* 93 (no. 5): 1118–1128.

13. Adam M. Grant and David A. Hofmann. (2011). "It's Not All About Me: Motivating Hospital Hand Hygiene by Focusing on Patients." *Psychological Science* 22, 1494–1499.

Notes

14. Adam Grant. "Ethical Systems." Ethical Systems, December 1, 2021. https://ethicalsystems.org/adam-grant/.

15. Adam Grant. "Ethical Systems." Ethical Systems, December 1, 2021. https://ethicalsystems.org/adam-grant/.

16. "BetterUp's New, Industry-Leading Research Shows Companies That Fail at Belonging Lose Tens of Millions in Revenue." BetterUp, n.d. https://www.betterup.com/press/betterups-new-industry-leading-research-shows-companies-that-fail-at-belonging-lose-tens-of-millions-in-revenue?utm_source.

Chapter 3

1. Alok Patel and Stephanie Plowman. "The Increasing Importance of a Best Friend at Work." Gallup, January 19, 2024. https://www.gallup.com/workplace/397058/increasing-importance-best-friend-work.aspx.

2. Patel and Plowman. "The Increasing Importance of a Best Friend at Work," January 19, 2024.

3. Leanne Italie. "Gallup: Just 2 in 10 U.S. Employees Have Work 'Best Friend' | AP News." AP News, February 7, 2023. https://apnews.com/article/workplace-friendships-poll-relationships-best-friends-office-faa0858e623e78c70e6f7eb02c55c7f1#:~:text=Just%202%20in%2010%20adult%20U.S.%20employees%20say%20they%20definitely,well%2Dbeing%20researcher%20Jim%20Harter.

4. Christine Porath and Carla Piñeyro Sublett. "Rekindling a Sense of Community at Work." *Harvard Business Review*, August 26, 2022. https://hbr.org/2022/08/rekindling-a-sense-of-community-at-work.

5. Rhitu Chatterjee. "Friendships at Work Can Boost Happiness. Here's How to Nurture Them." NPR, February 24, 2023. https://www.npr.org/sections/health-shots/2023/02/24/1158881773/friendships-at-work-can-boost-happiness-heres-how-to-nurture-them.

6. Liz Mineo. "Good Genes Are Nice, but Joy Is Better." *Harvard Gazette*, January 11, 2024, https://news.harvard.edu/gazette/story/2017/04/over-nearly-80-years-harvard-study-has-been-showing-how-to-live-a-healthy-and-happy-life.

7. Friday Pulse. "Why Teams Matter for Happiness and Success at Work | Friday Pulse," January 16, 2025. https://fridaypulse.com/insights/why-teams-matter-for-happiness-and-success-at-work.

8. Alex Pentland, Sociometric Solutions, and MIT. "The New Science of Building Great Teams." *Harvard Business Review*, April 2012, 1–17. https://www.agileleanhouse.com/lib/lib/Topics/Teams/The%20New%20Science%20of%20Building%20Great%20Teams.pdf.

9. Naomi Karina. n.d. https://www.msn.com/en-xl/africa/nigeria/80-great-collaboration-quotes-to-encourage-teamwork-and-unity/ar-BB1rdHaX.

10. "Cross-functional Teams May Boost Innovation, Adaptability," n.d. https://action.deloitte.com/insight/1892/cross-functional-teams-may-boost-innovation-adaptability.

11. Brian Uzzi. "Research: Men and Women Need Different Kinds of Networks to Succeed." *Harvard Business Review*, February 25, 2019. https://hbr.org/2019/02/research-men-and-women-need-different-kinds-of-networks-to-succeed.

12. Tracy Brower. "New Study: Making Friends Is Hard but Work Can Help." *Forbes*, October 5, 2022. https://www.forbes.com/sites/tracybrower/2022/10/05/new-study-making-friends-is-hard-but-work-can-help/.

13. Charlotte Nickerson. "Mere Exposure Effect in Psychology: Biases & Heuristics." *Simply Psychology*, October 10, 2023. https://www.simplypsychology.org/mere-exposure-effect.html.

14. Lito Lupena. "The Allen Curve—Thinkdev." Thinkdev, April 28, 2023. https://thinkdev.org/blog/the-allen-curve.

15. Terri Apter, PhD. "Why We Underestimate Others' Opinions of Us, and Why It Matters." *Psychology Today*, December 28, 2020. https://www.psychologytoday.com/ca/blog/domestic-intelligence/202012/the-liking-gap.

16. Ger Tillekens. "The Official Beatles' Canon," n.d. https://www.icce.rug.nl/~soundscapes/DATABASES/AWP/awp-beatles_canon.shtml#:~:text=Of%20those%2010%20performances%20most,a%20total%20of%20212%20songs.

17. Roy Williams. "Sinatra's Riddle: The Monday Morning Memo." Monday Morning Memo, August 20, 2024. https://www.mondaymorningmemo.com/newsletters/sinatras-riddle/.

18. Tom Geraghty. "Dunbar's Number, Psychological Safety and Team Size." *Psych Safety,* October 24, 2024. https://psychsafety.co.uk/psychological-safety-82-dunbars-number-and-team-size/.

19. Mark Cruth. "The Spotify Model for Scaling Agile | Atlassian." Atlassian, n.d. https://www.atlassian.com/agile/agile-at-scale/spotify.

20. Robin Dunbar. "Dunbar's Number." New Scientist, n.d. https://www.newscientist.com/definition/dunbars-number/.

21. Tonya Eckert. "Managers Impact Our Mental Health More Than Doctors, Therapists—and Same as Spouses." *UKG,* October 4, 2023. https://www.ukg.ca/about-us/newsroom/managers-impact-our-mental-health-more-doctors-therapists-and-same-spouses#:~:text=Managers%20impact%20employees'%20mental%20health,spouse%20or%20partner%20(69%25).

22. Marisa G. Franco, PhD. "'Openers' Are Masters at Getting Others to Open up. Let's Learn from Them." *Psychology Today,* October 30, 2019. www.psychologytoday.com/intl/blog/platonic-love/201910/5-ways-to-get-people-to-open-up-to-you?amp.

23. Thomas Oppong. "Complaining Rewires Your Brain to Make Future Complaining More Likely," theladders.com, February 13, 2020, accessed March 31, 2025. https://www.theladders.com/career-advice/complaining-rewires-your-brain-to-make-future-complaining-more-likely.

24. Alison Wood Brooks and Leslie K. John. "The Surprising Power of Questions." *Harvard Business Review,* May 1, 2018. https://hbr.org/2018/05/the-surprising-power-of-questions#:~:text=Alison's%20research%20reveals%20that%20participants,the%20person%20who%20answers%20questions.

25. Snipd. "Mastering the Art of Small Talk | 6min Snip from the Liz Moody Podcast," n.d. https://share.snipd.com/chapter/130e6b2d-cdca-4821-8aca-dd52a8c35776.

Chapter 4

1. Tifanny Sauber Millacci. "Master Resilience Training (MRT) in the US Army (+PPT)." Positivepsychology.com, November 28, 2017. Accessed March 20, 2025. https://positivepsychology.com/master-resilience-training-mrt/#:~:text=They%20use%20the%20US%20Army,the%20six%20competencies%20explained%20below.

2. Paul B. Lester. "Resilience Training in the U.S. Army." *Harvard Business Review,* October 19, 2010. https://hbr.org/2010/10/resilience-training-writ-large.

3. Paul B. Lester, et al. "The Comprehensive Soldier Fitness Program Evaluation Report #3: Longitudinal Analysis of the Impact of Master Resilience Training on Self-Reported Resilience and Psychological Health Data," US Army report, 2011. https://ppc.sas.upenn.edu/sites/default/files/csftechreport3mrt.pdf.

4. Jim Garamone. "Casey Visits Soldiers in Resilience Training," www.army.mil, July 22, 2011. https://www.army.mil/article/30534/casey_visits_soldiers_in_resilience_training.

5. Millacci. "Master Resilience Training (MRT) in the US Army (+PPT)."

6. Millacci. "Master Resilience Training (MRT) in the US Army (+PPT)."

7. Martin E.P. Seligman. "Building Resilience." *Harvard Business Review*, April 1, 2011. https://hbr.org/2011/04/building-resilience.

8. Arnie Cann, et al. "A Short Form of the Posttraumatic Growth Inventory." *Anxiety Stress & Coping* 23, no. 2 (July 6, 2009): 127–37. https://doi.org/10.1080/10615800903094273.

9. Daeun Park, et al. "The Development of Grit and Growth Mindset During Adolescence." *Journal of Experimental Child Psychology* 198 (July 3, 2020): 104889. https://doi.org/10.1016/j.jecp.2020.104889.

10. Stanford Teaching Commons. "Growth Mindset and Enhanced Learning." Teaching Commons, n.d. https://teachingcommons.stanford.edu/teaching-guides/foundations-course-design/learning-activities/growth-mindset-and-enhanced-learning.

Notes

11. Raquel Artuch-Garde, et al. "Relationship Between Resilience and Self-regulation: A Study of Spanish Youth at Risk of Social Exclusion." *Frontiers in Psychology* 8 (April 20, 2017). https://doi.org/10.3389/fpsyg.2017.00612.

12. Stanford Teaching Commons. "Growth Mindset and Enhanced Learning."

13. Fred Luthans, Gretchen R. Vogelgesang, and Paul B. Lester. "Developing the Psychological Capital of Resiliency." *Human Resource Development Review* 5, no. 1 (February 1, 2006): 25–44. https://doi.org/10.1177/1534484305285335.

14. Amy McKenna. "15 Nelson Mandela Quotes." *Encyclopedia Britannica*, n.d. https://www.britannica.com/list/nelson-mandela-quotes.

15. Zoe Wyatt. "Mind Matters: The Neuroscience of Workplace Resilience." *Neurology & Neuroscience* 4, 2023. https://www.sciencexcel.com/articles/Jord0dbxZlDWK4TmkMfW5bGaQw4YpolPH0pF8AUg.pdf.

16. Kelly McGonigal. *The Upside of Stress: Why Stress Is Good for You, and How to Get Good at It* (Penguin, 2016).

17. A.W. Brooks. "Get Excited: Reappraising Pre-performance Anxiety as Excitement." *Journal of Experimental Psychology General* 143, no. 3 (December 23, 2013): 1144–58. https://doi.org/10.1037/a0035325.

18. Arthur Kapetanakis. "Billie Jean King Reveals Origin of Iconic Quote: 'Pressure Is a Privilege.'" United States Tennis Organization, July 19, 2024, accessed March 20, 2025. https://www.usopen.org/en_US/news/articles/2024-07-19/billie_jean_king_reveals_origin_of_iconic_quote_pressure_is_a_privilege.html.

19. Alia J. Crum, Peter Salovey, and Shawn Achor. "Rethinking Stress: The Role of Mindsets in Determining the Stress Response." *Journal of Personality and Social Psychology* 104, no. 4 (February 25, 2013): 716–33. https://doi.org/10.1037/a0031201.

20. Michael Schrage. "How the Navy SEALs Train for Leadership Excellence." *Harvard Business Review,* May 28, 2015. https://hbr.org/2015/05/how-the-navy-seals-train-for-leadership-excellence.

21. Carl A. Castro, et al. "Battlemind Training: Transitioning Home from Combat," n.d. https://apps.dtic.mil/sti/citations/ADA481083.

22. Amy B. Adler, et al. "Battlemind Debriefing and Battlemind Training as Early Interventions with Soldiers Returning from Iraq: Randomization by Platoon." *Journal of Consulting and Clinical Psychology* 77, no. 5 (January 1, 2009): 928–40. https://doi.org/10.1037/a0016877.

23. Zara Abrams. "The Case for Kindness." American Psychological Association, October 29, 2024, accessed March 20, 2025. https://www.apa.org/news/apa/kindness-mental-health.

24. Eric W. Dolan. "Shared Music Experiences Enhance Pleasure and Boost Kindness, According to New Psychology Research." *PsyPost: Psychology News*, June 7, 2024. https://www.psypost.org/shared-music-experiences-enhance-pleasure-and-boost-kindness-according-to-new-psychology-research/#google_vignette.

25. Matthew Solan. "The Secret to Happiness? Here's Some Advice from the Longest-running Study on Happiness." *Harvard Health,* October 5, 2017. https://www.health.harvard.edu/blog/the-secret-to-happiness-heres-some-advice-from-the-longest-running-study-on-happiness-2017100512543.

26. "Selfless Volunteering Might Lengthen Your Life, Research Suggests." American Psychological Association, November 2011, accessed March 20, 2025. https://www.apa.org/monitor/2011/11/volunteering.

27. Ipsos and Oxford Economics. "Paid Time Off Trends in the U.S.," 2019. https://www.ustravel.org/sites/default/files/media_root/document/Paid%20Time%20Off%20Trends%20Fact%20Sheet.pdf.

28. Aflac WorkForces Report. "Workplace Benefits Trends: Employee Well-being and Mental Health 2022-2023," 2022. https://www.aflac.com/docs/awr/pdf/2022-trends-and-topics/2022-aflac-awr-employee-well-being-and-mental-health.pdf.

29. Shalene Gupta. "Your Employees Are Afraid to Take PTO, but a Third Are Playing Hooky from Work Anyway." *Fast Company*, May 21, 2024, accessed March 20, 2025. https://www.fastcompany.com/91128407/employees-play-hooky-work-pto-fear-survey.

30. Rebecca Zucker. "How Taking a Vacation Improves Your Well-Being," *Harvard Business Review*, July 19, 2023. https://hbr.org/2023/07/how-taking-a-vacation-improves-your-well-being.

31. Hilary Brueck. "What Taking a Vacation Does to Your Body and Brain." *Business Insider,* September 4, 2018. https://www.businessinsider.com/vacation-health-benefits-2018-8#researchers-who-followed-a-group-of-749-women-from-massachusetts-for-two-decades-found-that-those-who-went-on-vacation-less-than-once-every-six-years-were-nearly-eight-times-more-likely-to-develop-heart-problems-than-women-who-vacationed-twice-a-year-9.

32. Zucker. "How Taking a Vacation Improves Your Well-Being."

33. Anne Lamott. *Almost Everything: Notes on Hope* (Penguin, 2018).

34. Martin Seligman, et al. "Three Good Things." *PositivePsychology.Com*, n.d. https://www.kendal.org/wp-content/uploads/2021/02/Design-Your-Best-Day-Handout-Three-Good-Things.pdf.

35. B. Leipold and W. Greve. (2009). "Resilience: A Conceptual Bridge Between Coping and Development." *European Psychologist* 14(1), 40–50.

36. M.W. Voss, C. Vivar, A.F. Kramer, and H. van Praag. (2013). "Bridging Animal and Human Models of Exercise-Induced Brain Plasticity." *Trends in Cognitive Sciences*, 17(10), 525–544.

37. A.D. Ong, C.S. Bergeman, T.L. Bisconti, and K.A. Wallace. (2006). "Psychological Resilience, Positive Emotions, and Successful Adaptation to Stress in Later Life." *Journal of Personality and Social Psychology*, 91(4), 730.

38. A. Bandura. (1977). "Self-Efficacy: Toward a Unifying Theory of Behavioral Change." *Psychological Review* 84(2), 191.

39. G.A. Bonanno. (2004). "Loss, Trauma, and Human Resilience: Have We Underestimated the Human Capacity to Thrive After Extremely Aversive Events?" *American Psychologist* 59, no. 1, 20.

40. Jo Sweales. "How to Introduce a Learn-it-all Culture in Your Business: 3 Steps to Success." Microsoft Industry Blogs, United Kingdom, January 7, 2020. https://www.microsoft.com/en-gb/industry/blog/cross-industry/2019/10/01/introduce-learn-it-all-culture/.

41. "5 Questions on Hybrid Managers' Minds," n.d. https://www.microsoft.com/en-us/worklab/5-questions-on-hybrid-managers-minds#:~:text=The%20framework%2C%20called%20%E2%80%9C%20Model%2C,wellbeing%2C%20growth%2C%20and%20success.

Chapter 5

1. John Caddell. "Four Seasons Hotels Review a Daily 'Glitch Report.'" Futurelab.net, January 10, 2015. https://www.futurelab.net/blog/2015/01/four-seasons-hotels-review-daily-glitch-report/.

2. Rachel Botsman. *How to Trust and Be Trusted* (Pushkin Industries, 2025).

3. Botsman. *How to Trust and Be Trusted*.

4. "Groupthink." *Psychology Today*, December 3, 2024. https://www.psychologytoday.com/ca/basics/groupthink.

5. Team Mighty. "11 Gen. George Patton Quotes That Show His Strategic Awesomeness." *Military.Com*, March 29, 2022. https://www.military.com/history/2021/08/05/11-general-george-patton-quotes-show-his-strategic-awesomeness.html#.

6. Charles Duhigg. "What Google Learned from Its Quest to Build the Perfect Team." *New York Times*, February 25, 2016, accessed March 20, 2025. https://www.nytimes.com/2016/02/28/magazine/what-google-learned-from-its-quest-to-build-the-perfect-team.html.

7. Google re:Work. "Understand Team Effectiveness," n.d. https://rework.withgoogle.com/en/guides/understanding-team-effectiveness.

8. Amy C. Edmondson. *The Fearless Organization: Creating Psychological Safety in the Workplace for Learning, Innovation, and Growth* (John Wiley & Sons, 2018).

9. Ann Kowal Smith. "When Wrong Is Right: 5 Ways to Reframe Your Relationship to Failure." *Forbes*, November 27, 2023. https://www.forbes.com/sites/annkowalsmith/2023/11/27/when-wrong-is-right-5-ways-to-reframe-your-relationship-to-failure/.

10. Fearless Organization Scan. "Test the Psychological Safety in Your Team," n.d. https://fearlessorganizationscan.com/engage/test-the-psychological-safety-in-your-team.

11. Michael Distefano. "Alan Mulally: The Man Who Saved Ford," April 15, 2021. https://www.kornferry.com/insights/briefings-magazine/issue-20/alan-mulally-man-who-saved-ford.

12. Bill George, "The Massive Difference Between Negative and Positive Leadership." *Fortune*, April 24, 2021. https://fortune.com/2016/03/21/negative-positive-leadership-politics-ford-alan-mulally/.

13. Shauna O'Brien. "The Complete History of Ford: Income, Price & Dividends." Dividend.com, n.d. https://www.dividend.com/how-to-invest/the-complete-history-of-ford-f/.

14. Ed Catmull and Amy Wallace. *Creativity, Inc. (the Expanded Edition): Overcoming the Unseen Forces That Stand in the Way of True Inspiration* (Random House Canada, 2023).

15. Ed Catmull. "Inside the Pixar Braintrust." *Fast Company*, March 12, 2014, accessed March 20, 2025. https://www.fastcompany.com/3027135/inside-the-pixar-braintrust.

16. Wikipedia Contributors. "Pixar." Wikipedia, March 17, 2025. https://en.wikipedia.org/wiki/Pixar.

Chapter 6

1. Teresa Amabile and Steven Kramer. "The Progress Principle: Using Small Wins to Ignite Joy, Engagement, and Creativity at Work" (Harvard Business Press, 2011).

2. Teresa Amabile and Steven Kramer. "The Worth of Small Wins." American Management Association, March 24, 2020, accessed March 21, 2025. https://www.amanet.org/articles/the-worth-of-small-wins-teresa-amabile-and-steven-kramer-on-the-progress-principle/.

3. H. Liao, R. Su, T. Ptashnik, and J. Nielsen. "Feeling Good, Doing Good, and Getting Ahead: A Meta-Analytic Investigation of the Outcomes of Prosocial Motivation at Work," n.d. *Psychological Bulletin* 148, no. 3–4 (2022): 158–198. https://psycnet.apa.org/record/2022-80213-002.

4. Susan Sorenson. "How Employees' Strengths Make Your Company Stronger." Gallup, January 30, 2020. https://www.gallup.com/workplace/231605/employees-strengths-company-stronger.aspx.

5. Teresa Amabile and Steven Kramer. "The Power of Small Wins." *Harvard Business Review*, May 1, 2011. https://hbr.org/2011/05/the-power-of-small-wins.

6. H. A. Simon. "Rational Choice and the Structure of the Environment." *Psychological Review* 63, no. 2 (1956): 129–138. https://psycnet.apa.org/record/1957-01985-001.

7. Shahram Heshmat. "Satisficing vs. Maximizing," *Psychology Today*. June 13, 2015. https://www.psychologytoday.com/ca/blog/science-choice/201506/satisficing-vs-maximizing.

8. Sheena S. Iyengar and Mark R. Lepper. "When Choice Is Demotivating: Can One Desire Too Much of a Good Thing?" *Journal of Personality and Social Psychology* 79, no. 6 (January 1, 2000): 995–1006. https://doi.org/10.1037/0022-3514.79.6.995.

9. David Rock. "Humans Are Mentally Checked Out, Unhappily, Nearly Half the Time." *Psychology Today*, November 14, 2010. https://www.psychologytoday.com/ca/blog/your-brain-work/201011/new-study-shows-humans-are-autopilot-nearly-half-the-time.

10. Talya Minsberg. "How to Accomplish a Huge Goal (One Step at a Time)," *New York Times*. November 5, 2024, accessed March 21, 2025. https://www.nytimes.com/2024/11/01/well/how-to-achieve-goals.html.

11. Albert Bandura. (1977). "Self-efficacy: Toward a Unifying Theory of Behavioral Change." *Psychological Review* 84(2), 191–215. https://psycnet.apa.org/record/1977-25733-001.

12. Sabina Nawaz. "To Achieve Big Goals, Start With Small Habits." *Harvard Business Review*, January 20, 2020. https://hbr.org/2020/01/to-achieve-big-goals-start-with-small-habits.

13. Amabile and Kramer. "The Worth of Small Wins."

14. Amabile and Kramer. *The Progress Principle*.

15. A.C. Shilton. "You Accomplished Something Great. So Now What?" *New York Times*, May 28, 2019, accessed March 21, 2025. https://www.nytimes.com/2019/05/28/smarter-living/you-accomplished-something-great-so-now-what.html.

16. Minsberg. "How to Accomplish a Huge Goal (One Step at a Time)."

17. Minsberg. "How to Accomplish a Huge Goal (One Step at a Time)."

Chapter 7

1. Lee Mohon. "Apollo 13: The Successful Failure," *NASA* (blog), June 23, 2023. https://www.nasa.gov/missions/apollo/apollo-13-the-successful-failure/.

2. Wikipedia Contributors. "Failure Is Not an Option." Wikipedia, March 4, 2025. https://en.wikipedia.org/wiki/Failure_is_not_an_option.

3. Jeff Haden. "43 Years Ago, 'Star Wars' Creator George Lucas Made a $4-billion decision—Even Though It Had Nothing to Do with Money," Inc.com, January 6, 2020, accessed March 24, 2025. https://www.inc.com/jeff-haden/43-years-ago-star-wars-creator-george-lucas-made-a-4-billion-decision-even-though-it-had-nothing-to-do-with-money.html.

4. Charles S. Carver, Michael F. Scheier, and Suzanne C. Segerstrom. "Optimism." *Clinical Psychology Review* 30, no. 7 (February 2, 2010): 879–89, https://doi.org/10.1016/j.cpr.2010.01.006.

5. Lewina O. Lee, et al. "Optimism Is Associated with Exceptional Longevity in 2 Epidemiologic Cohorts of Men and Women." *Proceedings of the National Academy of Sciences* 116, no. 37 (August 26, 2019): 18357–62. https://doi.org/10.1073/pnas.1900712116.

6. Linda A Bressler, Mark E Bressler, and Martin S Bressler. "The Role and Relationship of Hope, Optimism and Goal Setting in Achieving Academic Success: A Study of Students Enrolled in Online Accounting Courses." *Academy of Educational Leadership Journal* 14 (January 2010): 37–51, https://www.researchgate.net/publication/282613197_the_role_and_relationship_of_hope_optimism_and_goal_setting_in_achieving_academic_success_a_study_of_students_enrolled_in_online_accounting_courses.

7. Martin E.P. Seligman et al. "Positive Psychology Progress: Empirical Validation of Interventions." *American Psychologist* 60, no. 5 (July 1, 2005): 410–21. https://doi.org/10.1037/0003-066x.60.5.410.

8. Naman Gopal Srivastava. "'My Goggles Filled Up with Water'—Michael Phelps Swam Blind for Over 175m to Achieve One of His Biggest Career Achievement." EssentiallySports, June 6, 2022. https://www.essentiallysports.com/us-sports-news-swimming-news-my-goggles-filled-up-

with-water-michael-phelps-swam-blind-for-over-175m-to-achieve-one-of-his-biggest-career-achievement/.

9. Tchiki Davis. "Visualization Can Help You Reach a Range of Goals," *Psychology Today*, November 20, 2023. https://www.psychologytoday.com/intl/blog/click-here-for-happiness/202308/how-visualization-can-benefit-your-well-being.

Chapter 8

1. Saul McLeod. "Fundamental Attribution Error in Psychology." *Simply Psychology*, June 15, 2023. https://www.simplypsychology.org/fundamental-attribution.html.

2. Leanne Italie. "Gallup: Just 2 in 10 U.S. Employees Have Work 'Best Friend.'" AP News, February 7, 2023. https://apnews.com/article/workplace-friendships-poll-relationships-best-friends-office-faa0858e623e78c70e6f7eb02c55c7f1.

Chapter 10

1. Uncommon Business. "#3: Ari Weinzweig, Co-founder of Zingerman's Community of Businesses, Author, Philosopher, and Anarchist." Buzzsprout, February 4, 2024. https://podcast.uncommon.fm/2230716/episodes/14438689-3-ari-weinzweig-co-founder-of-zingerman-s-community-of-businesses-author-philosopher-and-anarchist.

2. Wayne Baker. "Zingerman's Community of Businesses: A Recipe for Building a Positive Business." Harvard Business Publishing Education, May 17, 2013. https://hbsp.harvard.edu/product/W88C61-PDF-ENG.

3. Wayne Baker. "Zingerman's Community of Businesses: A Recipe for Building a Positive Business."

4. Elizabeth Hotson. "Is This the Sweet Secret to Swedish Success?" February 25, 2022. https://www.bbc.com/worklife/article/20160112-in-sweden-you-have-to-stop-work-to-chat.

5. Ministry of Foreign Affairs of Japan. "Special Feature on Schools in Japan: Classroom Duties." Web Japan, n.d. https://web-japan.org/kidsweb/cool/21/202101_on-duty-activity_en.html.

6. Motoko Rich. "Documentary Filmmaker Explores Japan's Rigorous Education Rituals." *New York Times*, April 5, 2024, accessed March 25, 2025. https://www.nytimes.com/2024/04/05/world/asia/japan-documentary-films-ema-ryan-yamazaki.html.

7. Alexandra Huetter. "What Is Borrelen? The Dutch Art of Going for a Drink with Co-workers." *DutchReview*, September 12, 2024. https://dutchreview.com/expat/work/borrelen/.

8. Fabien D'Hondt et al. "Explicit and Implicit Emotional Processing in Peripheral Vision: A Saccadic Choice Paradigm." sciencedirect.com, July 14, 2016, accessed March 25, 2025. https://www.sciencedirect.com/science/article/abs/pii/S0301051116302472.

Acknowledgments

Thank you to my friends and family, who put up with me throughout this very long process! I promise I will talk about something else now. And thank you to my many coaches who helped me along the way. You all know who you are and I appreciate each and every one of you!

About the Author

With over 15 years of experience, Jessica Weiss brings a unique blend of scientific research and practical business acumen to her work. She has helped Fortune 500 companies, tech startups, and everything in between to cultivate thriving workplace cultures that drive success.

Jessica has witnessed firsthand the toll of stress and burnout on both individuals and organizations. She became passionate about finding a better way to achieve success without sacrificing well-being.

This led her to develop her groundbreaking "Happiness, Works" methodology. Today, Jessica is a sought-after speaker, author, and trusted advisor to leaders who understand that happy employees are the key to a flourishing business. For more information, please visit www.jessicaweiss.com.

Index

External motivators, reliance, 7–8

External validation, evidence, 8

F

Failure
    acceptability, 101–102
    handling (setback), 164–168
    script, rewriting, 165
    transformation, 165–166
    visibility, 171
Favoritism, 93
Fears, acknowledgement/ reframing, 104
Feedback, 174, 191
    process, trust, 107–108
    sharing, 144–145
    transformation, trust (impact), 107
Fields, Mark, 103
Fixer, role, 57–58
Fredrickson, Barbara, 10–11
Friends
    attraction, 46–47
    having, importance, 40–45
    making, 33–34, 39, 46–57
Friendship, 60
    secret, 184–186
Fulfillment, progress (impact), 126
Future-casting, 162

G

Game-changer, usage, 112
Gender, influence/imbalance, 45
Glitch, recovery, 86
Glitch Report, 85–87, 213
    meeting, 101–102, 108–109
Glueck study, 16
Goals
    selection, 126–127
    small size, thinking, 131
Grant, Adam, 32
Gratitude
    display, 151
    fatigue, fighting, 145
    gift, 144–145
    positive emotion, 11
Great Renegotiation, 2
Grit/perseverance (growth factor), 66
Groupthink, 99
Growth, challenges (impact), 66

H

Happier Hour (Holmes), 12
Happiness, 60. *See also* Work happiness
    action, 153
    blue zones, identification, 20
    broaden and build theory, 10–11
    build, time (usage), 13
    choice, myth, 9–11